FUN ACTIVITIES TO DO WITH YOUR KIDS

167 CREATIVE PROJECTS, GAMES AND CRAFT IDEAS YOUR CHILDREN WILL LOVE

ROB PLEVIN

http://www.liferaftmedia.com

http://www.liferaftmedia.com

Print ISBN: 978-1-913514-18-1
Kindle ISBN: 978-1-913514-19-8
eBook /other ISBN: 978-1-913514-20-4

YOURS FREE:

TWO 'Kid's games' MINI-GUIDES as a thank you for buying this book.

'10 Fun Travel Games to Play with Your Kids'
'10 Fun Garden Games to Play with Your Kids'

Just visit the following page on my website and you'll be able to download them immediately.

GO HERE RIGHT NOW TO GET YOUR FREE COPIES:

www.liferaftmedia.com/10fun

CONTENTS

INTRODUCTION

If you've ever been stuck for ideas for spending quality time with your child, this is the book for you. You'll find it a satisfying workout for your *'Super Parent'* skills: an inspiring resource of games, ideas, activities and learning experiences – but most of all FUN – that can be set up indoors, and sometimes out of them. I hope you'll return to plunder it again and again. Some games need virtually no preparation or materials, and some will have you planning ahead and raiding the craft box and kitchen cupboards.

These activities can be undertaken at any time, not just on school holiday. It can be after school, on a rainy weekend, when you've had a last-minute change of plan, when you just need to get the darlings from under your feet for an hour – or even when a nasty virus has you all locked indoors and *Super Parent* has to add some home-schooling into the mix. And that's why many of the activities in this 'recipe for fun' book incorporate some social skill-building.

Sometimes children just want to get on with things on their own, and sometimes they need your help and involvement. Sometimes you will be happy to leave them while you get on with your grown-up stuff, and sometimes the child in you will take over and you'll be elbowing your way into the fun. And I can guarantee you'll have that – all the activities herein have been tested to make sure they work. I am a father myself, but had an eager pool of friends' and neighbours' kids to draw on for games that required testing with greater numbers.

Don't forget that you're not just providing entertainment and education – you're building lasting memories. When you think of your favourite film you don't think of the two hours it takes you to watch it – you remember how it makes you *feel*. That's why you read and re-read your favourite books. It's the same with shared experiences: *'Hey, kids, remember that time when...'* and you do remember that time, because you had such fun together. You'll be greeted with a lot more enthusiasm than if you ask 'remember that time you watched that thing on the iPad...'

Anyway, that's enough from me. It's time to get stuck in. Before you know it you'll have your children happy, active, creative, and busily making memories. And please – don't worry when things don't go to plan. That's when you can have the most fun!

QUICK AND EASY ACTIVITIES

Before we get into the more creative type of activities with step-by-step instructions that require a little planning (but not too much, I promise), I've put together some quick lists of go-to activities that will keep children happily entertained for at least 5 minutes.

So if you're short on time and need something fun and super-easy to just grab and go, check out this list of some top child favourites:

CLASSIC GAMES

- Articulate
- Boggle
- Charades for Kids
- Chess
- Checkers
- Cluedo
- Connect Four
- Dominos
- Enchanted Forest
- Game of Life
- Guess Who
- Happy Families
- Jenga
- Jumanji

CLASSIC GAMES *(continued)*

- Kids vs Parents
- Ludo
- Mouse Trap
- Monopoly
- Operation
- Pictionary
- Rapidough
- Scrabble
- Snakes and Ladders
- The Chase
- Top Trumps
- Twister
- Uno
- Yahtzee

QUICK INDOOR ACTIVITIES

- Bake together
- Create a holiday brochure or postcard to learn about another culture, or a place they have always wanted to visit
- Fix a bike or repair a puncture
- Plant veggies or flowers
- Play 'shops' to learn about currency, buying, and selling
- Practice first aid together and role-play a nurse's or doctor's office where the 'patients' are teddy bears, dolls, or even you
- Role-play a game that utilises your phone number so that they can remember it in case of emergencies
- Build with LEGO
- Colouring Books
- Jigsaws

QUICK INDOOR ACTIVITIES *(continued)*

- Cook a Meal Together
- Create a Word Search
- Dominoes
- Have a Disco
- Learn to Sew or Knit with Online Tutorials
- Make a Blanket Cubby
- Make a Poster
- Make Models with Play Dough
- Have a Movie Night with popcorn
- Paint by Numbers
- Pillow Fight
- Play Board Games
- Print Photographs and Organise a family photo album
- Read together

QUICK OUTDOOR ACTIVITIES

- Build a simple 'duvet and chairs' den in garden
- Put a tent up in the garden
- Go on a bug hunt
- Create a Slip 'n' Slide
- Fill the Paddling Pool and have a water fight
- Have a Picnic
- Hide 'n' Seek
- Learn to Cartwheel
- Make a Fire Pit and Roast Marshmallows
- Play Hopscotch
- Set up a Lemonade Stand
- Sketch an Outdoor Scene
- Go on a Bike Ride
- Go on a Long Walk as a Family (or even a fun, short one just around the block)
- Play tennis or football
- Play catch with a ball
- Trampoline to Music and/or Bubbles, or (our favourite) - with the sprinkler underneath

ARTS AND CRAFTS

These days there's a plethora of art and craft kits on the market, and you can really save your money by not buying them! There's no end to the projects your child can get creative with independently, or together with you – with materials you probably already have at home.

I bet you have paper, cardboard, sticky tape, pencils and markers – and an imagination too. If not, don't worry; I have ideas that are easy and fun... and not *too* messy. And if you don't have any of those things, just pop by your local art and craft supplies store or buy online using one of the suppliers at the end of this chapter.

ALPHABET GAME

What you'll need: A3 piece of paper or sugar paper; a ruler; a pen; coloured pens.

1. Draw up a large table, as big as will fit on the paper, with four columns and 26 rows (children will probably need your help with this). Then get them to work (while you have a coffee) making it 'cool' with stickers, glitter, paints, or whatever they like.

2. Down the left-hand column write all the letters of the alphabet. Then, above the remaining three columns, think up categories together of things they love such as *'Pets', 'Princesses', 'Superheroes', 'Sports'*.

3. Now challenge your children to see if they can fill all the cells in the table using the matching letters of the alphabet. If they're stuck let them use a dictionary or the internet.

   To make it more exciting, you can time them or award points for faster completion – they are sure to love the challenge.

   Another variation could be to pop one of these up on the wall after the activity is done, and let them complete one cell each morning – great for building vocabulary.

CREATE A LEGOLAND

What you'll need: A large cardboard box; a heap of Lego; white paper; colouring pencils or pens.

1. Take your large box and cut off the top flaps and one of the larger sides. You'll need to be on hand to help with this part.
2. Tell the children that even though they can't visit the real thing yet, they're going to build their very *own* miniature Legoland. Ask them what kinds of things they'd expect to see, like rides, kiosks, dinosaurs etc. Make a list.
3. They will have a lot of fun building the structures for their own park, as well as using their pens or pencils to add grassland, rivers, paths, and roads. I find those long rolls of plain white paper handy for this; they can just roll out the length they like.
4. Once they've finished preparing everything, they've got their very own Legoland to play in and it's ready to go for future role-playing games.

CARDBOARD BOX BUILD-A-THON

What you'll need: A whole heap of cardboard boxes; stickers; colouring pens or paints (if you're feeling brave); cushions; box cutters or scissors; blankets.

1 While it's fun to make a fort with cushions, a few cardboard boxes can really fire up the creative urge of children. Once you clear enough space, they can create a vehicle, a castle, or an entire pirate ship – they are really only limited by their imagination.

2 Help the children get started, handling the box cutters or scissors to break down boxes wherever needed. If you're ambitious – and don't need the room anytime soon – you could create something huge that takes up the entire room. They'll love it for weeks.

3 Once the structure is complete, they can decorate the exterior and interior using stickers or colouring pens, add props, or make it feel cosier with cushions and blankets. For a pirate ship, you could even add a sail using a sheet or blanket. Make sure you bring out the dress-ups so they can really be a part of their new world.

(If you have a *lot* of space, time, and an abundance of thick cardboard boxes you just don't know what to do with, take a look at the film *Ant-Man and the Wasp*.)

CARDBOARD CATS

What you'll need: Colouring pens or pencils; some cardboard (A4-sized is fine); a pair of scissors; some glue (Sellotape will work).

1 Have your child draw a simple cat's body shape onto a piece of cardboard from top to bottom; lend assistance as required. If you don't have cardboard, just cut out one panel from a cereal box.

2 To create the legs, cut two parallel lines up the centre of your cat's body to slightly below the halfway point. You're going to want these several centimetres apart depending on the width of your cat. This flap you've created will be your cat's legs.

3 Fold the bottom half of this leg flap forward about a couple of centimetres; these are the paws. Then fold the same amount of card backward on the cat's main body.

4 Cut out the shape of a head, plus two separate ears and a tail. Get them creative; make them wavy, folded, stuck-up, whatever they like. Glue them all onto your cat's body and head – or use folded Sellotape if there's no glue in the house.

5 With colouring pens or pencils, fill in some basic detail for the body, head, tail, and legs. If you're making

more than one cat, they can get creative and make a variety of cats, drawing in some lighter stomach patches, cute facial markings, or pretty collars.

6 Use white paper to cut out the cat's eyes and some strips for the whiskers, then glue these into place on the head. Draw a pupil in for the eyes, too. Meow!

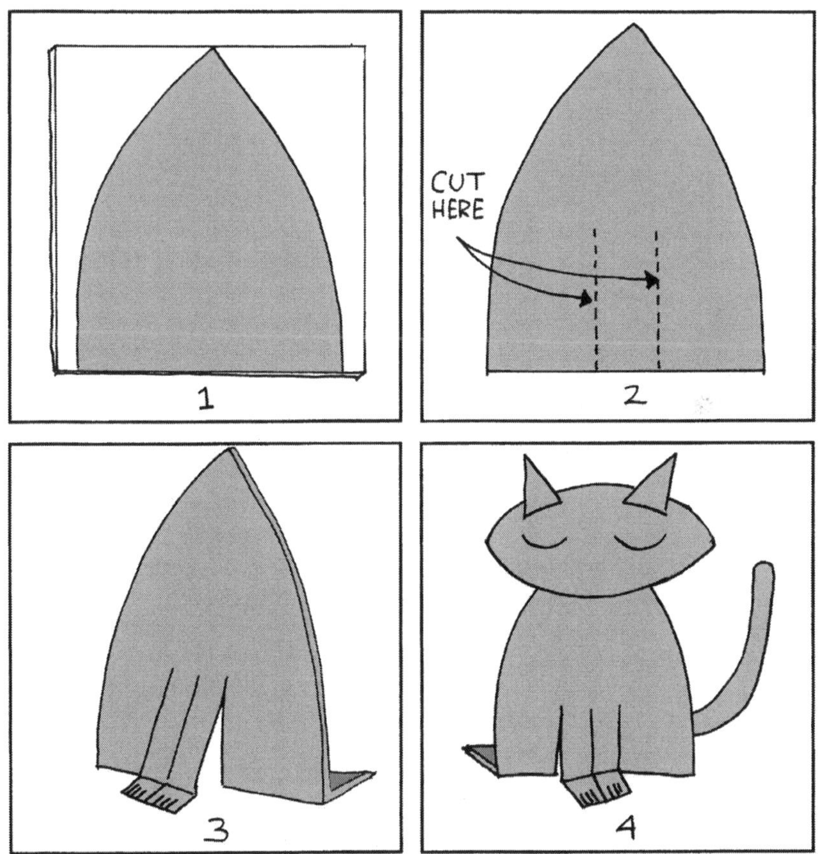

CARDBOARD DINOSAURS

What you'll need: Cardboard; scissors; black felt tip marker.

1 Have your child draw two shapes out on the cardboard; one for the body, neck, and tail, and another two matching shapes for the legs as shown in the image.

2 Let them cut out a series of spikes from scraps of cardboard. While the shapes should be the same, the sizes can be slightly different so that the spikes decrease in size as they go down the dinosaur's back.

3 Next cut slits into the dinosaur's body along its back and all the way down to the tail. Then, cut a slit into the bottom of each spike and slot it into place on the body or tail until they're running all the way down from head to tail.

4 Cut some toe shapes into the base of each dinosaur foot, then cut two slits on the underside of the dinosaur and one slit on top of each pair of legs. Slot the legs onto the body, and the dinosaur is ready to come alive! So get the children decorating their dinosaur with colouring pencils, pens, or paints, or they could

shred tissue paper and stick it on using PVA glue for a more textured looking animal.

Now it's time to play. Get ready for the ROAR! and STOMP! of dinosaurs.

CARDBOARD MICE

What you'll need: Toilet roll tube(s); pastel chalks; thin cardboard and paper; glue.

1 Start with your toilet roll tube. Fold in half a thin piece of card and then cut out the shape of a mouse's nose. Cut the shape out while the card is folded and glue the tips together, then glue the back of the nose to the toilet roll tube.

2 Using paper, cut out some shapes for the mouse's eyes and ears, then choose a place for them near the nose – the crazier the better. You can also cut out whiskers to attach to the mouse's nose.

3 Cut out a rectangular strip of paper and glue it around the body of the tube, creating a t-shirt or sweater – so cute! This can be coloured in and designed too. Then, cut out some arms and hands and glue them to the body, colouring the arms in the same colour scheme.

4 Cut out two feet using the thin cardboard again and add some lines for toes. Then, cut two slits into the bottom of the toilet roll tube and slot the feet in. Now can the mouse chase the cat?

CARDBOARD MICE *(continued)*

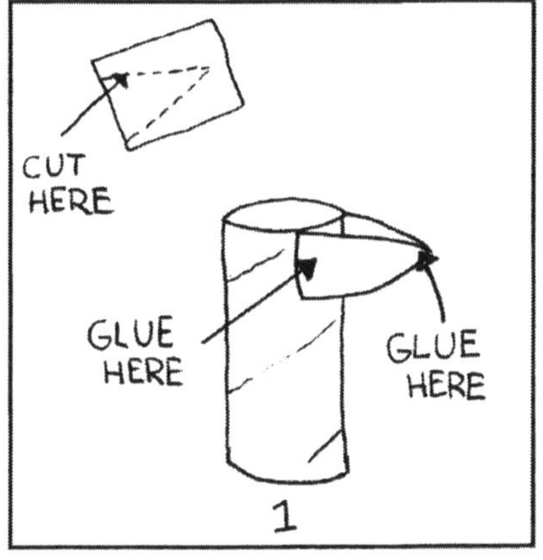

DESIGN (AND SWAP) A WORD SEARCH

What you'll need: A4 paper; pens or pencils; a ruler; a dictionary (optional).

1 Ask your children to mark out a grid on a piece of paper using a pen or pencil and a ruler, and check that it covers most of the page; but leave room for words to be written outside the grid, at the side and/or bottom.

2 Have them come up with a list of around ten interesting/fun or silly words (or more if there's space) and write them into the grid. They can use a dictionary if they want to, though make sure they don't try to make it overly tricky.

3 Move onto filling the remainder of the blank spaces with random letters. Finally, list all the words included in the word search down the side of the grid, or in the blank space beneath.

DESIGN (AND SWAP) A WORD SEARCH *(continued)*

4 Finally, they can swap word searches with one another and try to complete them. Or, if you have one child (like me) they could work on this activity at the same time as a friend (or yourself) and then swap photos with each other to complete. They can also be swapped over the internet with friends or family members who don't live close by. Another way to keep connected!

DIY CRAYONS

What you'll need: Various colours of crayon; silicone ice cube trays.

If your home is anything like mine your crayon collection will be full of cracked, broken or worn-down fragments that have seen better days – but for which you can still find a use...

1 First tear off any remaining wrappers then break the crayons into smaller pieces. Then lay them in the silicone trays. You can keep the colours separate, but mixing some together 'in the name of research' can definitely add a scientific edge to crafting fun – and your *Super Parent* status is enhanced!

2 Place your silicone trays into the oven and bake them at around 200 degrees for 10 to 15 minutes. Make sure you're using trays designed for that heat, or you will end up with something unusable from Frankenstein's toy lab.

3 Your crayons should now have melted down, at which point you can slide the trays into the freezer until they set. Then hey presto – your kids are getting creative with brand-new crayons that they made themselves!

DIY FOAM PAINT

What you'll need: Shaving foam; PVA glue; Ziplock bags; a pencil; some food colouring in different colours; a large piece of thin or thick cardboard.

If this sounds messy – it is.
But when has mess ever got in the way of fun?

1 Mix equal parts of PVA glue and shaving foam into a Ziplock bag. Have them stir and then drop in some food colouring and then seal the bag. Then let them have fun shaking and squashing the bag around until the ingredients are fully mixed.

2 Using a pencil, get your children to sketch out a layout for their picture on the card or cardboard. They can use these sketches as guidelines for their paint colours.

3 When their guidelines are in place, just chop off a small corner of the Ziplock bags and use them to pipe paint onto the picture. They'll love this, it's like piping icing onto a cake. When they're done, set aside the pictures overnight to allow the paint to set.

DIY MARBLE RUN

What you'll need: Marbles; duct tape; empty kitchen roll and toilet roll tubes; scissors.

I had heaps of fun as a child setting up complex marble runs and watching the little glass balls tumble through the tubes. With this activity, your child can set up something as long and complex as they can imagine.

1 Choose a wall that won't get ruined by a little duct tape – or use something that's strong but less harsh on paint when removed. I prefer to set this up on outside walls or in the garage.

2 Cut small square or rectangular 'entrance holes' into one side of one of the ends of your tubes. When the marbles fall, they'll need to fit through these holes, so don't make them too small or it will be a big fail and you won't be popular!

3 Using your tape, stick the tubes to the chosen wall in a series of tunnels, so that when you drop marbles into the first tube at the top, they cascade down through the maze of tubes. Now, the most important bit – grab your coffee, sit back, and relax while they giggle and play for ages.

DIY MARBLE RUN *(continued)*

FAMILY TREE

What you'll need: Recent ancestors/family (pre-made); pencil or pen; A4 paper; ink pads (several yellows and greens).

1. Start by helping the children sketch a large tree, which covers the whole of your paper. Copy an image from the web or print one out, ensuring there are plenty of branches – enough for all the family members, maybe even great- great- great-ones.

2. Have them use their thumbs in the ink pads, then press them against the paper along each branch, creating a mix of yellow and green cute thumbprints for the leaves. This makes your tree even more personal and special – indeed unique! If you don't have ink pads, you could use a small amount of acrylic paint in a dish instead. Warning – while *we* love the family tree idea – *they* will probably love this painty bit the most.

3. Start by writing the names of the oldest relatives you know within your family at the foot of the tree, on either side of the trunk. You could always prep for this activity by using one of those online family history websites to find out more (or perhaps unearth skeletons!).

4 Teach your little ones about each member of the immediate and extended family, then have them add the family members to the branches as they extend upwards and outwards, with the youngest members at the top and cousins and uncles on opposing branches. I guarantee you will all feel connected after this activity and they will remember it for many years to come.

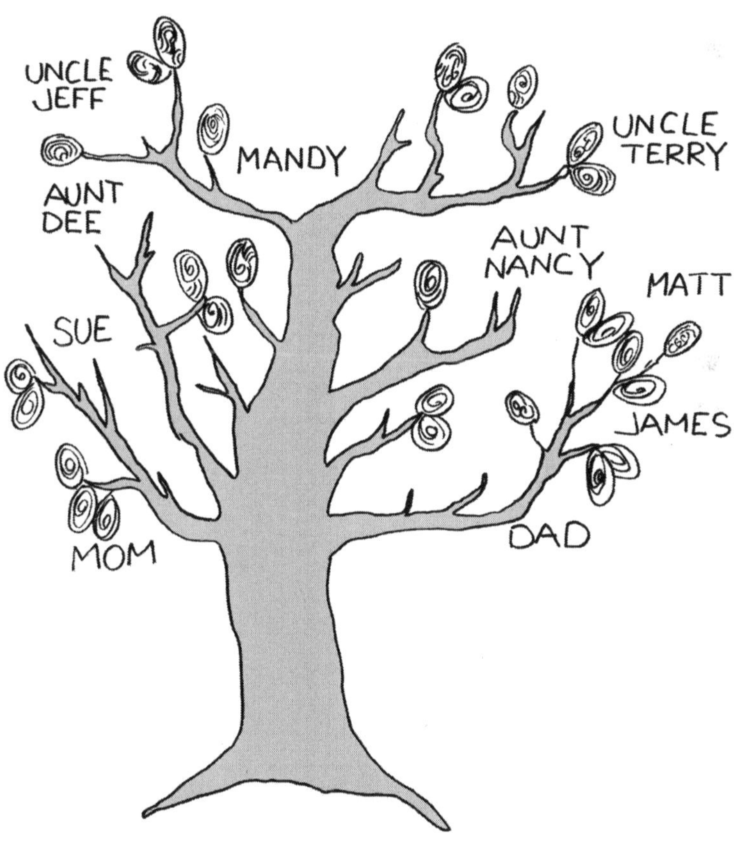

FOIL AND PAPER BIRDS

What you'll need: Kitchen foil; paper (tissue paper works best); PVA glue; scissors; thin card.

1 Take a large sheet of tin foil and help your child scrunch it up into a bird shape; you should end up with a fat body, a protruding shape for the head, and a tail tapering off at the end. Don't worry if it's not anatomically accurate – it won't be!

2 Children will love starting to shred up paper for the feathers. Tissue paper works well, but you could also use newspaper or even simple A4 paper in different colours. Once that's done (and you've plucked the 'feathers' from yours and your child's hair) spread PVA glue over the tin foil and have your children press the 'feathers' into place.

3 Next – you may need to help with this – fold a small piece of thin card in half, then cut a triangular shape out of it for the beak. Glue it into place on the bird's head.

4 Using the card again, cut out two wide shapes for the feet, then glue them to the bottom of the bird so that it can stand by itself. Cool or what? The only thing left to do is to draw or paint on a pair of eyes; sticking on some small pieces of white paper or little pompoms also work well here.

FOIL AND PAPER BIRDS *(continued)*

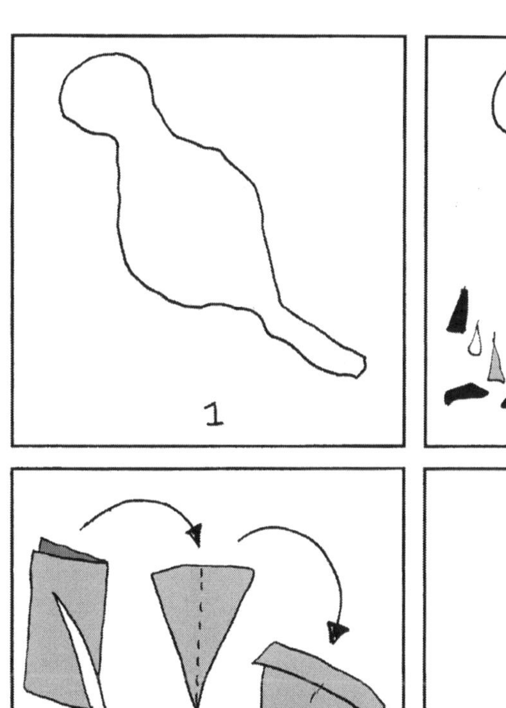

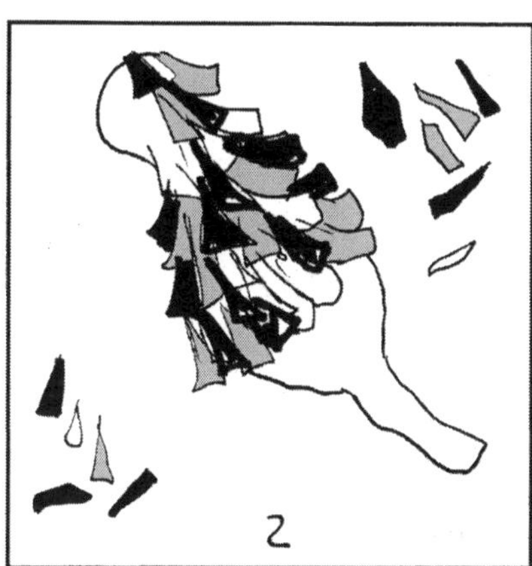

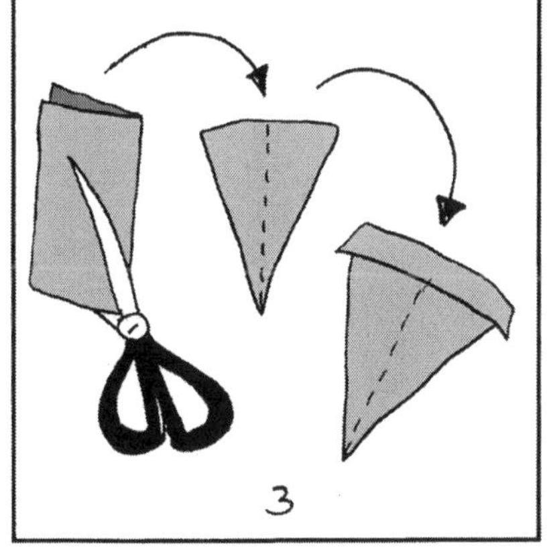

LANTERNS FROM JAM JARS

What you'll need: Various sizes of glass jars; tissue paper in different colours; scissors; PVA glue; battery-operated LED lights; ribbon.

1 Start by cleaning off the glass jars – jam jars, pickle jars, anything will do (be warned – the children will use this as an excuse to finish off any jars with goodies inside). Get them to help soak the labels off and remove any sticky label residue, then dry them out thoroughly.

2 Have your children tear up the tissue paper into small squares around 2 to 3cm. It doesn't matter if they're rough around the edges; they will love this part so allow extra time for this.

3 Start to spread a thin layer of PVA glue around the outside of the jar, making sure that all sections of the glass are covered. Then go section by section, applying overlapping pieces of tissue paper.

4 Once the whole exterior of the jar is covered, fold some tissue paper over so it's thicker and hide the rim using the same technique.

5 Finish the jars off by pasting another layer of PVA across all of the tissue paper to seal it, then leave to dry for a couple of hours. (The children will be checking them every minute – to hurry this up, pop them in sunshine if you have any). When they're done, tie a ribbon around the rim to pretty them up or to personalise.

6 The final, exciting step is to insert a battery-powered LED tealight into each jar. The great thing about these jars is that you can keep them around for ages, unlike other more quickly-forgotten crafts.

MAKE A MUSICAL INSTRUMENT – GUITAR

What you'll need: A large cereal box; a cardboard tube (e.g. kitchen roll); scissors; rubber bands; duct tape (or strong Sellotape); a pencil.

It might not sound like real music to your ears, but it will be real music to theirs. I don't need to tell you that children love making noise, and this activity could keep them entertained and dancing about for a while – as well as feeling pretty proud of themselves.

1 Cut a large circular hole in one side of the cereal box, just slightly off-centre (towards the top of the box where the opening is). If you want a bigger guitar, use a bigger cereal box. If you wanted a smaller guitar... just kidding, you get the idea. If there is one major art and crafts ingredient that's never in short supply, it's typically cereal boxes (or Amazon etc, if you shop a lot online.)

2 On the top side of the cereal box, where the opening is, create small slits along the side of the box that you've created the hole on.

MAKE A MUSICAL INSTRUMENT – GUITAR *(continued)*

3 On the bottom side of the cereal box, hold your cardboard tube in place, and help your child stencil around the outline with a pencil. Then, help cut around the stencil using scissors to create a second hole in the box.

4 Cut small slits into the cardboard tube at one end, then wedge the other end of the tube into the smaller hole you created on the cereal box. Secure this into place with tape so that it can't move.

5 Wrap rubber bands from the slits you created at the top of the 'guitar neck' (the cardboard tube) to the slits you created at the bottom of the 'guitar body' (the cereal box). Now put on some favourite tracks and get them to play along while you get some tidying done. Did I say tidying? Forget that – call a friend, read a book, or eat some chocolate.

MAKE A MUSICAL INSTRUMENT – TAMBOURINE

What you'll need: 2 paper plates; paint and a brush; strong glue; uncooked lentils or rice; sequins; a hole punch or pencil; 4 short lengths of ribbon; 4 small decorative bells.

1 Start by having your child paint the back of each plate with a few coats. If you've got sequins, now is the time to glue them on to get the tambourine sparkly and musical once the paint is dry.

2 This is the fun part. Pour the dried rice or lentils onto one of the plates (make sure the paint and glue have fully dried) leaving some space for it to move around. Then, apply the strong glue around the rim and seal the two plates together.

3 Once the glue has set, punch a hole through four corners of the tambourine – you can use a pencil here if you don't have a hole punch – and help your child thread the ribbon through one bell for each corner, then through the holes you've created. Tie a knot to keep them in place, and you're done. Shake it, shake it, baby!

MUSICAL JARS

What you'll need: A collection of around 5 or more empty jars of a similar size and shape (ideally the same size and shape); spoon; water; optional dye.

1 This one can be done indoors or outdoors. Line up your jars. Have your child tap each jar with a spoon and notice how they all sound quite similar. Next help your child fill each jar with varying levels of water. For extra fun, add a little food dye into each jar for a visual flourish.

2 Now have your child tap each jar and see their surprise as they notice how different they all sound. Maybe they could make up a little song! They can write the colours down – for example: 'Red, red, blue. Red, red, blue. Red, red, red, red, red, red, blue.' I know what you're thinking – catchy!

PAPER BUTTERFLIES

What you'll need: Scrap paper; a pencil; scissors; glue; pipe cleaners; colouring pencils.

1. Have your child fold two scraps of paper in half, then open them out and draw one pair of butterfly wings across each folded piece, with the seam running down the centre where the butterfly's body would be.
2. Under your supervision have the child cut along the lines you've drawn so that they're left with two pairs of butterfly wings. Your child can then bring it to life by drawing patterns and designs directly onto the wings. Make it pretty!
3. When they've finished drawing, they can glue the top wing onto the bottom wing so that they're slightly overlapping. All that's left to do is to add the body; pipe cleaners work perfectly for this and can be glued into the centre of the wings where the fold is.
4. If they have fun with this, you can create a whole kaleidoscope of butterflies that look completely different (yes, a group of butterflies really is called a kaleidoscope). Use different colours of paper and different coloured pipe cleaners. They could even incorporate some of the finished butterflies into other activities, like a collage or picture.

PAPER BUTTERFLIES *(continued)*

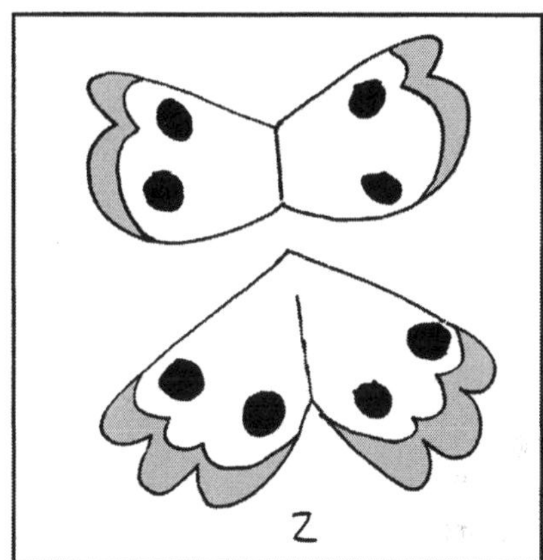

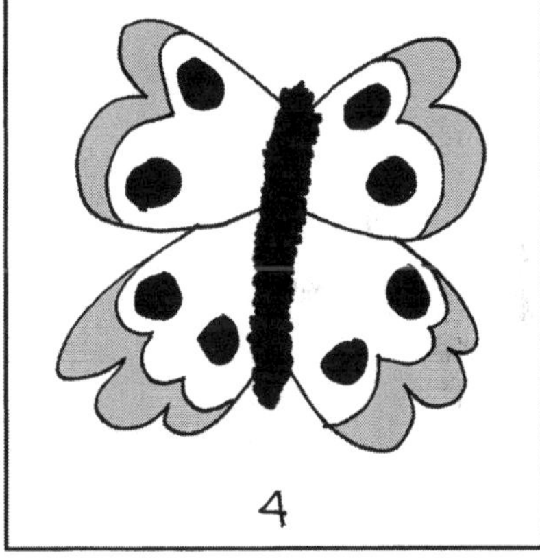

PAPER PLANE COMPETITION

What you'll need: A lot of A4 paper and thin card; some cardboard boxes; a sharpie marker.

1 Start by helping them to fold a whole range of planes together. You can use online templates to make a huge variety of planes with different wings, flaps, tails, and various thicknesses of paper or card.

2 Close the flaps on your cardboard boxes and then cut holes of various sizes into the bottom of them. Next, write point values beside the holes on each box – more points for smaller holes and fewer points for larger ones. Then, place these strategically around the room.

3 Your children need to take their squadrons of planes and try their best to land them into the holes cut into the boxes from the other side of the room. Go on, have a go yourself!

4 You can mix this up further with other competitions. For example, whose plane can do the most loops in a single throw? Whose plane can fly the furthest in a straight line? Who can land one on sleeping dad's head?

PIPE CLEANER FINGER PUPPETS

What you'll need: Pipe cleaners; pom-poms; googly eyes; a glue gun.

1 To begin, wrap a pipe cleaner around your child's finger three to four times, ensuring you leave around half of the pipe cleaner unwrapped at the end. Not too tight.

2 Fold that straight end over on itself once, creating an ear, then leave a small space and do the same for the other. You should now have two 'ears' above the coiled section of pipe cleaner.

3 Glue one pom-pom into the place where the two ears intersect – this will also keep your puppet together and stop it from unwinding.

4 Attach googly eyes to the front of the pom-pom and you've got yourself a super-simple finger puppet. Experiment with colours, goofy stick-on teeth, and other props, or bend the ears in different ways.

PORTRAIT KEY RINGS

What you'll need: Shrink plastic; colouring pencils; scissors; permanent marker pens; a hole punch; a metal key ring.

1 Mark a small square on your shrink plastic, roughly 15cm by 15cm. This will be the area they can draw in, to create their own self-portrait. So, get them to draw their own portrait inside this square then colour it in with pens or pencils.

2 Cut the square out with scissors leaving a small border, then punch a hole through the top of the picture, a few millimetres from the edge. Once that's done, bake the plastic in the oven as per the instructions on its packaging. I *loved* doing this as a child. It's quite amazing to watch it shrink.

3 Once their plastic keyring has hardened and cooled all that's left to do is to attach a key ring. You can do a lot with these; for example, you could create a keyring with their pet's picture, or create sports equipment, food items or favourite book or movie characters, even hang them from their school bag.

PORTRAIT KEY RINGS *(continued)*

SNAIL MAIL TO FAMILY

What you'll need: Lined paper; envelopes; stamps; colouring pens or pencils (optional).

1 Tell the children they're going to write some 'snail mail' – real letters with stamps, to a family member or friend. Younger children (or parents!) may not believe that this is how we had to communicate.

   I find it helps to give them some ideas of what to write about – a recent fun day out; something exciting they are looking forward to; a story they have written or picture they have made; how they feel about different things. And make sure they remember to ask the addressee how they are too.

2 Once it's done, they could also colour, use stickers, and pictures for the envelope.

3 Have your children fold their letter and slot it into the envelope, then add a stamp (delivering another short history lecture while doing so?) and write out the name and address. While they will have fun with this, it's also an educational activity that will help them with their writing and grammar skills.

'THANK YOU' CARDS

What you'll need: Thin A4 card; white paper; paints and a brush; painter's tape; scissors; some glue.

1 Let your children go wild with the paints on a piece of A4 paper – they'll love it. Don't worry if the patterns get a little messy as we're going to cut them up. Meanwhile, fold out a piece of A4 card as the basis for your greetings card.

2 Take the dried paintings and help to cut shapes out of them that can be stuck down into a pattern. At Christmas, you could create a Christmas tree from cut-outs, but for a thank you card, you could use a heart, a flower, or spell out a message.

3 Let them arrange the pieces into a fun pattern or message first, then once you've got the final design down, use the glue to stick them in place.

For a quicker activity, you can use painter's tape or washi tape to create a word or phrase on the front of your card (e.g. 'Thank You'). Then let them go nuts with the paints, and once you peel away the tape, you'll have a thank you message spelled out against a colourful background with minimal room for error.

STORY STONES

What you'll need: A handful of small pebbles (you can often find smooth white ones from craft or hardware stores); coloured permanent markers; a paintbrush; white acrylic spray paint (optional); gloss craft varnish.

1 You don't strictly need to spray the stones white, but this is the first step if you have the white spray paint. Spread them across newspaper outdoors, spray them all, moving onto the reverse side once dry. This will make the pictures 'pop' much better.

2 Using the permanent markers, have them draw a picture on each of the pebbles – this could be things like fairytale characters, trees, butterflies, or other animals, vehicles, and food. All the things they love.

3 Once they're done, the final touch is to apply a fine layer of gloss varnish over the pebbles to seal in the colours, add a little shine, and make them last.

4 We keep our stones in a little pouch, a bag is fine. Take turns taking out a stone and make up a story with each stone adding to the storyline. You'll be surprised at what you all come up with. I've also found the stories give a little insight into what's important/of interest to the child at the time, or if something is on their minds.

STORY STONES *(continued)*

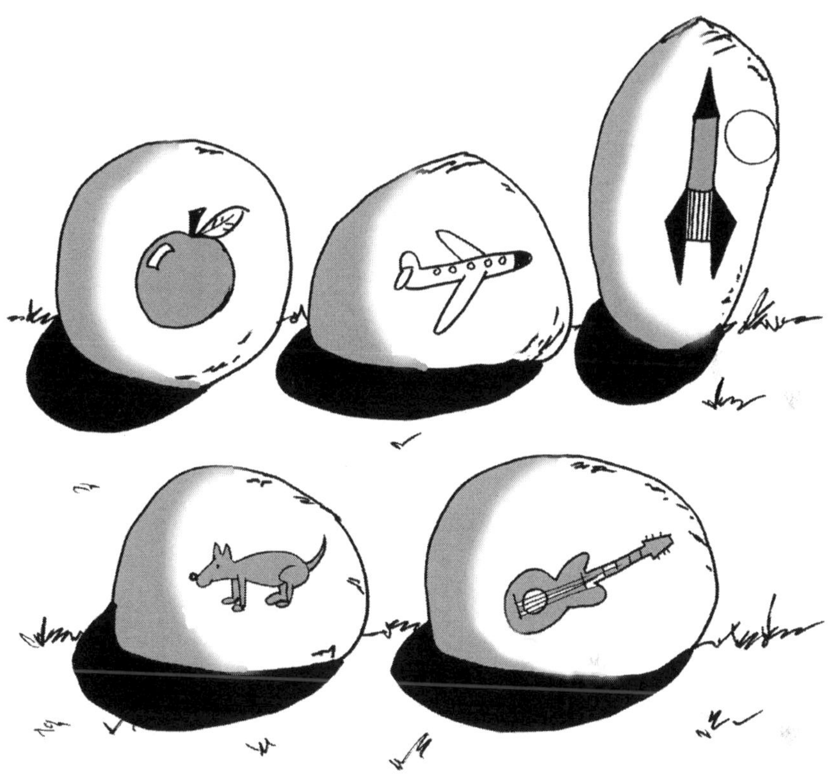

TOUCH AND FEEL BOXES

What you'll need: Several empty boxes (shoe boxes are perfect); scissors; paint and brushes or coloured pens; your choice of mystery objects to place inside.

1 Take your boxes or shoeboxes and cut a hole in the middle of each lid, leaving enough room for your child's hand to fit through.

2 Let the children get creative with paint or colouring pens, creating their own designs on the box and the lids.

3 Make them cover their eyes and choose some mysterious objects to put inside the boxes, using a different object for each one. You could use simple things like pipe cleaners, tissue paper, or objects from the garden – anything. Or if you're feeling brave try messy, fun stuff, like cooked spaghetti, passion fruit, peeled grapes, or jelly! Bear in mind that messy things may also make a mess of the box.

4 Finally, the fun. Line the boxes up in a row and let your children take turns in reaching into each box to guess what's inside – wait for the squeals. Once they've guessed them all, have a stash ready because they are going to want more, and more.

LOOKING FOR SOMEWHERE TO GET YOUR CRAFT SUPPLIES?

We consider the following companies to be the best suppliers of arts and crafts materials. They each have a huge range of materials and also provide wonderful crafting ideas & techniques on their websites and social media channels.

United Kingdom (with worldwide online ordering)

Hobby Craft

www.hobbycraft.co.uk

Starting more than 25 years ago in 1994, Hobby Craft is now the largest arts and crafts retailer in the UK. As well as supplying materials for just about every crafting activity you could think of – including art, crochet, haberdashery, papercraft, baking, jewellery making, clay modelling and much more besides.

Hobby Craft also provide more than 1,500 easy-to-follow tutorials on a huge variety of crafting techniques and have a very active, free membership – the Hobby Craft Club. Members receive exclusive offers, ideas & guidance in special techniques.

United States & Canada (with worldwide online ordering)

A Cherry on Top

www.acherryontop.com

A Cherry On Top Crafts began in a little shoe box full of stickers more than 20 years ago and now carries thousands upon thousands of products including paper crafts, general crafts, needle arts, sewing & quilting supplies, art supplies, and so much more.

Their site features a gallery where you can share your projects and ideas and you can also join their crafty community and learn new techniques by chatting on their message boards or signing up for their free newsletter.

Exclusive Reader-only discount...
Get 10% off when you use this code: 'RPTEN'

BALLOON ACTIVITIES

There are just so many balloon activities that they had to have their own section.

BALLOON BADMINTON

What you'll need: A few balloons; 2 or more paper plates; duct tape; long craft sticks (or just sticks).

1 Start by helping the children tape a long craft stick to the back of two paper plates, (craft sticks are like lollipop sticks, just longer; a regular lolly stick will be too flimsy and short here). If you don't have craft sticks, you could use a strong twig from the garden, but the flatter the better.

2 Blow up a few balloons – one to play with and some others as backup. Balloons sometimes pop easily so it's handy to have a few extra on hand.

3 If you've got some time (and patience) you can mark up some lines on the ground for the boundaries of the court. My girl loves to bat the balloon back and forth without any net or markings, but if yours are super competitive, the court markings mean you can keep score and nominate a winner at the end.

BALLOON HOCKEY

What you'll need: No shortage of balloons, a kid-size hockey stick (or a rolled-up newspaper).

1 Set up some goalposts at opposite ends of the room – I use a laundry basket tipped on its side (the washing can wait) or you could use a large cardboard box.

2 Move anything breakable and let the children battle it out to see who can score the most points. Award points every time they manage to knock the balloon into the net.

BALLOON ROCKET RACING

What you'll need: Some balloons; scissors; drinking straws; string; tape; clothes pegs.

1. In the garden or on the deck (or indoors if you can't go out or don't have outdoor space) string up two lengths of string as far across as you can manage, spaced some distance apart. Make sure that the strings are at a kid-friendly height.

2. Tie one end and then thread a straw onto both lines at the opposite end, before tying those up, too. This could be to a fence or taped to an indoor wall if you're doing it inside.

3. Blow up a balloon and clamp it shut with a clothes peg to keep the air in. Then, tape one side of the balloon to the straw. Do the same for the straw on the other string using a second balloon.

BALLOON ROCKET RACING *(continued)*

4 Move away breakable objects. With one kid holding each balloon, count down from 3 and then have them release their pegs. Woohoo! Watch the balloons whizz down the line as they race to the finish.

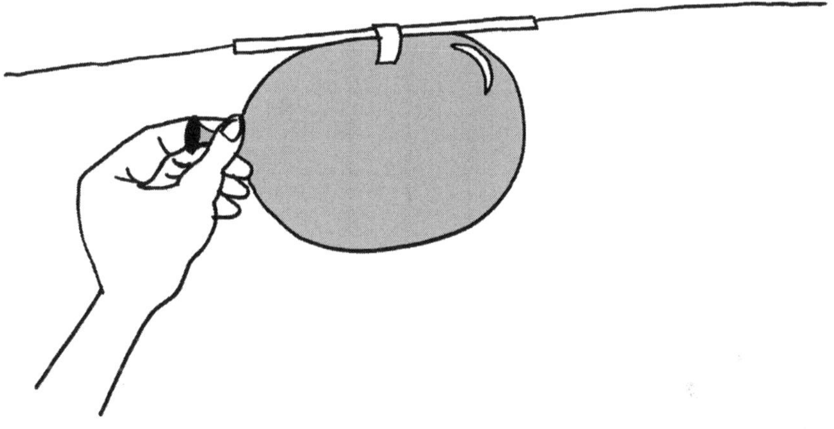

BALLOON PAINTING

What you'll need: Several balloons; acrylic paints in various colours; sugar paper; paper plates.

1 Get ready for some messy, sensory fun using nothing but balloons and paints. Start by blowing up several balloons with your child – enough so that you've got one for each colour of paint. Also, squeeze out some paint onto paper plates, using one for each colour so that it's easily accessible. I would recommend doing this outside, but if you're indoors put down a craft mat or newspaper first.

2 Show them how it's done. Dip the rounded surface into the paint and then use them to make circular shapes on the sugar paper.

3 Let them go wild with the balloons and paints. See what shapes they can come up with. Just watch out for balloons getting popped accidentally – trust me, I've been there and you don't want to be painting anywhere near treasured furniture if one of these things pops.

BALLOON PIÑATA

What you'll need: A bag of balloons; chocolates, sweets or miniature toys; something to jab the balloons with.

1 Start by blowing up loads and loads of balloons – without the children seeing, squeeze a sweet or wrapped chocolate into each balloon before you fill them. You could also use small toys such as you'd find in Christmas crackers. Anything will do if it fits and doesn't have sharp bits.

2 Set up your balloons; how you do this depends on the size of the task and the 'pointy thing' you're going to use to pop them. You could use darts, if you're able to keep a close eye and if they're a bit older, with the balloons pinned to a piece of plywood out in the garage. Or, you could arm the family with relatively pointy sticks and fill a room with balloons – some filled with treats filled and some empty.

3 Once your children have been equipped with the weapons of choice, block your ears, then set them loose on the balloons and let them go until they've all been popped. They'll love the surprises.

BALLOON VOLLEYBALL

What you'll need: Duct tape; string; a newspaper; some balloons.

1 String up a length of string across the lounge or another room, from one wall to another. This will form the top of your volleyball net, so don't make it too high for the children.

2 Take your newspaper apart and hang sheets all along the string – and voila, you have a net. If you want it to be more lifelike or easier to see through, you could fold your sheets over twice and cut pieces out of the fold to give the newspaper sheets a more net-like appearance.

3 Once you've got your net, you are good to go. Use your balloons in place of a ball to save the breakables and tally the scores on a chalkboard or piece of paper.

'BLOW THE BALLOON' RACE

What you'll need: A bag of balloons, some electrical tape (optional).

1 Blow up several balloons – one for each child (and for you if you're joining in); do a couple of spare ones since some are bound to pop.

2 Mark up a course through your home using electrical tape, though if you don't have any you can just explain the course and use things like sofa cushions to block off doorways not in use. Create narrow chicanes by blocking off sections of the hallways, or ramps by laying thin plywood over smaller sections of stairs. If you involve the garage in the course, you could even set up some water obstacles to make things even more exciting.

3 Now for the game: the children have to get onto their hands and knees and blow the balloon along the course. The first person to get their balloon across the finish line is the winner. And, you know, this is also a great way to sneak a good core, arm, and upper body workout into their fun – while you watch!

DIY BALLOON DROP

What you'll need: A tablecloth; a few bags of balloons; some confetti; pens; sweets or chocolates; around 10-inches of string; a hole punch.

I should point out before you start that this activity must involve a tablecloth you don't want any more – because it's going to be cut in half. So put grandma's heirloom safely away.

1 Let the kids cut your cloth in half, if they can – they'll love to chop up a big household object without fear of punishment! You will end up with two squares (don't worry if they're not exact squares).

2 Along the cut edge of both squares of tablecloth, punch holes equally spaced apart by around an inch.

3 Have your child thread the string through the holes as if they're lacing their shoes, though not too tightly. Make sure there's plenty of leftover string hanging down from one end once you're done, as this will be your ripcord.

4 Hang your creation from the ceiling; duct tape works quite well here. Just make sure that when it's in place, there is some slack in it, as you'll need space for the balloons.

DIY BALLOON DROP *(continued)*

5 Blow up as many balloons as you can manage before your lungs collapse, the more the merrier. In secret, fill some of them with small treats, chocolates or miniature toys. Write simple maths problems onto pieces of paper and insert them into others. Draw pictures onto several of them. You can do all these things separately, but the idea here is that when you pull the cord, your children should try to grab as many balloons as they can.

6 When you pull the cord and they've grabbed as many balloons as possible, it's time to see what they've caught. Depending on how you've set up the balloons, they can pop them to find out whether there are treats inside. If they get a simple maths problem, they've got to solve it. If you're using balloons with pictures, they can come up with a story on the spot using the balloons like story stones.

MEGA BOUNCY BALL

What you'll need: Round water bombs or balloons; tap water.

With this activity your child will have one of the bounciest bouncy balls around. And it won't take anything more than a pack of water bombs (or balloons) and some tap water

1 Start by filling one of the balloons with just enough water that it stretches out a little, then tie it off and cut away the excess rubber above the knot.

2 Help your children to cut the heads off of the rest of the balloons or water bombs while they're empty.

3 Being careful not to pop the water-filled balloon, squeeze it inside of one of the empty balloons from which you've already removed the head. Make sure the knotted side is facing inwards. Continue pushing the main balloon inside of empty ones, until you have a thick layer of rubber around the ball from all the empty balloons.

MEGA BOUNCY BALL *(continued)*

4 Each time you add a few layers, get your children to give it a bounce, and see how high it can fly. Once you're satisfied with the super orbital power of the ball, you can stop adding new layers and they can go crazy seeing how high it'll bounce, and hopefully it won't go over the fence. We all know bouncy balls eventually disappear into a black hole, but these are so easy to make that goners are easily replaced.

PROTECT THE BALLOON

What you'll need: A bag of balloons; some lengths of string (around a metre long).

This activity works great when you've got around 4 or more people.

1 Start by enlisting the child's help to blow up a balloon for everybody who's playing. Make sure you choose an area where there are no sharp objects for them to fall onto.

2 Tie a balloon to each player's ankle with the lengths of string. Don't tie it too tightly, but make sure it's not going to slip off if they're running and jumping around.

3 Now get them running and jumping around. The goal here is to smash everybody else's balloons before yours gets smashed. You're going to want to supervise in this game to stop them getting too out of control (as it can get) but this game focuses on what children do best – having fun!

HIGH-ENERGY ACTIVITIES

This section is bursting with energy. It's full of activities geared towards those times when the children seem to get suddenly restless or hyper. For me, it's usually when mine is impatiently waiting for a friend to arrive, when a tantrum is brewing, right before bedtime, or sometimes it's just out of the blue.

These activities will help to burn off that excess energy, or at the very least create a distraction. I find it's not a bad idea to join in myself as I find that it reduces a bit of tension built up by the situation. And afterward, we're always feeling more connected. Other times, once you've set up the activity, they'll be able to continue by themselves while you get on with other things.

ACTIVITY DICE

What you'll need: Printable dice template; computer; printer; blindfold.

1 Search for a printable dice template online that you can use to create your own dice; the six sides should be blank for you to edit. You could do this by hand or on the computer using a photo-editing software program.

2 Create two or three dice of your own. One should be a 'time dice', with sides set up to show *'15 seconds'*, *'30 seconds'*, and *'45 seconds'* for example. Create another with physical activities, like *'jump'*, *'sit-ups'* or *'planking'*. You could also create a third with restrictions, such as *'blindfolded'*, *'silently'* or *'one hand tied behind the back'*.

3 When you're ready to play, your children take turns rolling the two or three dice. Then they act out whatever action lands face-up, for the amount of time shown on the face-up time die. Trust me, a *lot* of that energy will be released after this.

ACTIVITY DICE *(continued)*

4 You can easily build on this activity by creating different sets of dice. For example one set of dice could show different exercises; each morning, everyone in the family could roll the dice and complete one exercise together. You could create some dice that have all the household chores on them. If you have several children, you could even throw in something like *'20 minutes of video games'* on one of the die's faces. This way, they'll have that bit more incentive to roll the dice – especially if there's a chance they get to kick back and relax while their siblings wash dishes or do the dusting!

CONVERT THE GARAGE

What you'll need: Outdoor toys; water balloons; skipping ropes; anything else they like to use outdoors.

1 Start by clearing out your garage, moving old boxes, vehicles, dozing grandparents, and anything else that might get in the way.

2 Bring all your children's outdoor toys inside the garage so that they have a safe space to use them without leaving the house. As it's the garage, you could give them things like water balloons or water pistols, providing you've moved anything that could get damaged.

   They will *love* this. It's amazing how the same toys in a different space can make them all exciting again.

3 If you want to build in some exercise, you could set up a small climbing frame inside the garage or hang some climbing ropes or ladders. Your children will love playing around with a load of their outdoor toys or climbing all over these things, especially if they're stuck indoors. You could even make an obstacle course.

FOLLOW THE DRUMMER

What you'll need: Makeshift drumsticks (chopsticks, sticks, long markers); drums (stack of boxes, pots, and pans); optional earplugs.

1 Set up several drum stations, one for each of your children – and for yourself if you're taking part (like I do) – using pots, pans, boxes, or anything else you can find.

2 Choose who's going to be leading the activity; you could demonstrate first. The first person to go must thump out a drum solo that the others are going to follow.

3 Move onto the next person, who has to repeat the same tune. You can start with shorter beats before moving onto longer ones if you want to ramp up the difficulty.

FUNNY FASHION SHOW

What you'll need: A range of colourful clothes; shoes, hats, scarves or glasses; cool music.

1 Gather together a haul of clothing – these can be the children's clothes or some of yours if you have anything from last season you don't mind being tossed around. You can also use shoes, scarves, glasses and anything else you think might be fun.

2 Clear out some space in the lounge and move the chairs around to create a catwalk area. Your children can take it in turns selecting an outfit to put together for the catwalk. Make sure you crank up some catwalk-like music so they can really strut their stuff.

3 When they're strutting (and you're busily taking photos because they look so cute) the others can announce what they've chosen. *"This is Millie, she's wearing a lovely red summery dress and matching shoes"*, or something like that – you get the idea.

GIANT FLOOR MAZE

What you'll need: Coloured electrical tape in various colours; a pen and some paper; some treats or mini snacks; a toy or button for the kids to move through the maze.

1 Lay out a large square of electrical tape on a hard floor; this will be the boundary of your maze, so remember to leave an entrance and an exit or they'll be stuck forever.

2 Start to apply lines inside of the boundaries, creating your passageways through the maze. Make sure to add lots of dead ends along the way. One path should, of course, lead from the entrance to the exit.

3 In some of the dead ends, add a healthy snack or other treat. Write out a question or maths problem that they must solve before they get the treat, or write a riddle. Time them through the maze and see who can get through fastest – though they'll probably be tempted to dash for the snacks first.

INDOOR BOWLING

What you'll need: Electrical tape; large red cups; a medium-sized ball; a chalkboard and chalk (or pens and paper) for scoring.

1 Start by marking two long 'gutters' down the side of your hallway or living room using electrical tape.

2 Set up a tower or triangle of red cups at the end of the alleyway you've created.

3 Have your children take turns bowling (you can take part too) and keep track of scores on the chalkboard or paper, with one knocked-over cup scoring one point. You can have a prize for the highest scorer at the end.

4 You can liven this up and make it feel more like a real bowling alley by serving a meal like hot dogs, nachos or burgers – and if the weather's good enough for a BBQ, even better.

LEGO BRICK HUNT

What you'll need: A wide range of Lego pieces in different sizes and four to five different colours; paper or card matching each of the colours you're using.

1 I don't know one kid that does not love a treasure hunt. Start by laying out a piece of paper in the same colour as each of your Lego brick pieces – so if you're using red, green, blue, and white pieces, you'll need four sheets of paper in these colours.

2 Hide your stash of Lego pieces throughout the room or the house, depending on how much space you want to use for the activity.

3 Start timing and let your children hunt down the Lego pieces you've hidden, returning them to their corresponding paper colours. Make sure you tell them how many pieces they're looking for.

OBSTACLE COURSE

What you'll need: Cushions; plastic cups; hula hoops (large toys, not the crispy snack); long strips of crepe paper or thick duct tape; electrical tape; balloons; table and chairs – and any other household items you want to include.

1 Start by putting together an intricate maze in one of your hallways or living room. Using electrical tape to hold down the edges, weave lengths of crepe paper or duct tape from one side of the hall to the other. Create a maze that the children will have to carefully crawl, duck, and weave through; don't make it too easy.

2 From here, work your way outwards creating more obstacles. Set up a series of couch cushions for your children to use to hop from one to the next.

3 Create a small tunnel or maze using your dining table and chairs and any sheets or blankets you have spare.

4 Use the plastic cups to create a course your children have to run through or weave around.

This is just a general idea, but there are endless ideas you can use here to make the obstacle course as long as you want it to be, provided it's safe.

OBSTACLE COURSE *(continued)*

SARDINES

What you'll need: Nothing!

1 This is a twist on an old favourite, hide and seek. Nominate the child (or person) who is going to be hiding first. Everybody else is going to be on the opposing team.

2 When the game starts, everyone else has to count to the agreed number and then hunt down the kid that's hiding. If somebody finds them, instead of the game ending, they've got to try and squeeze into the same hiding place. So prepare to be squished!

3 The game continues until everybody in the 'finding' team has located the hiding spot and squeezed in alongside everybody else – just like a tin of sardines, but hopefully without the funny smell. Encourage trying to find hiding spots that aren't too small so that the game can continue for longer.

STICKY NOTE BEAN BAG TOSS

What you'll need: Sticky notes; a pen; a pile of bags or soft balls.

1 On the back of a closed door stick 26 sticky notes and write one letter of the alphabet on each of them. Let the children do the writing if they can (good writing practice task set by *Super Parent!*).

2 Mark out a line on the floor several feet away from the door (gauge the distance on the child's age and height) and tell them they can't step forward beyond this line.

3 Next, have them toss bean bags or a soft ball at the letters to spell out a word of your choosing. Balled-up socks or stuffed toys can be thrown, but hide the family pet before play starts, if it's a small one.

STICKY TAPE SPIDER WEB

What you'll need: Sticky tape or electrical tape; balloons; newspapers.

1 Start by stringing lengths of sticky tape across a doorway opening, with the sticky side facing the play area. You're making a web.

2 Help scrunch up a handful of newspaper balls – they'll stick the easiest – or use small balloons for a little extra challenge. Toss them into a container or stack them beside the play area.

3 Now toss the balled-up newspaper or balloons at the spider's web and give points to them when they succeed. If you want to make it educational, write points values on the balloons and have them tally up their score as they go.

TAPE CAR TRACK

What you'll need: Various colours of decorator's tape (red, grey, yellow); cardboard; toy cars; an unused corner of the room.

1 Start by setting out some boundary areas in the corner of the room – your 'city limits'. Box off the area using some coloured masking tape. Then, create some 'parking spaces' along the edge of the boundary area that your children can use to park their vehicles when they're done playing.

2 Lay down some roads within the 'city' using grey or white masking tape. Create roundabouts, junctions, and pedestrian crossings using another colour of tape like the yellow.

3 Fold your cardboard over into the shape of a tunnel and place it over a stretch of road, then secure it to the floor with some tape to make your cityscape a little more interesting.

4 If you have Lego lying around, they can be added to the city with buildings and other obstacles. The great thing is, if this is a relatively unused corner of a playroom, the city can remain in place for future play sessions whenever a distraction is needed, plus you can expand it even further in the future.

TIMELINE OF MY LIFE

What you'll need: Large piece of paper (the long rolls of paper are great for this as you can make your timeline as long as you like); colored pens and pencils; ruler.

1 Start by having your child write the heading, 'Timeline of My Life'. Next help them mark out even intervals on the bottom of the page. These will be the major milestones of your child's young life.

2 Underneath the milestone marks, label the year. There will be one special milestone for each year. We usually do around 7 years.

3 Brainstorm the most major or special moments of that year; you may need to prompt your child here with some ideas. Have them draw and describe that special milestone. These are just adorable and you will want to keep this forever. Some special milestones could be: birth of sibling, first pet, new home, special visitors, exciting holiday, starting school, mastering a skill such as learning to ride a bike, learning to read... or first cartwheel!

WORD GAMES

WHO/WHAT AM I?

What you'll need: Nothing!

1 This is a great game to play anywhere – at home, perhaps while you're making dinner or some other task, or in the car, or waiting somewhere. First, you can start by imagining someone or something, and keeping it in your mind.

2 Next have the young ones guess who or what it is by asking questions. Each question is met with a yes or a no, helping the child get closer to the solution. Then it's time to swap over and it's your turn to guess. This is a simple but surprisingly entertaining game.

I WENT TO MARKET AND...

What you'll need: Nothing!

1 As above, this is a great game to do at home, perhaps while you're making dinner or some other task, in the car, or waiting somewhere. First, you can start by one person saying 'I went to market and bought... a banana.' The next person carries on adding an item up to the list, 'I went to market and bought a banana, milk...' See how long your list can get!

TALK FOR A MINUTE

What you'll need: Some flashcards (cut out from thin card or paper); a stopwatch or other timer (voice assistants are great); a pen or pencil.

1 The setup is straightforward. On a stack of blank flashcards, use either pictures or words to create a stack of single-word objects or subjects. You can grade these for age, but off the top of my head, you could use things like: *'sports', 'food'* or *'school'*. If your children are into a particular tv show, you could use the character's name.

2 Set the cards down at the front of the room, face-down, and have each of your children go up to pick a card from the pile. If you're playing with one child, you can get involved too – show them how it's done.

3 Once a card is picked up, the player has to speak for a minute on whatever topic the card displays. Just wait for the cute things they come out with.

4 If you want to get competitive you can award points – for example, 50 points for a perfect score without stopping. Minus 10 points for repeating facts. Minus 10 points for pausing. Minus 10 points for repeating

TALK FOR A MINUTE *(continued)*

'err' or saying filler words like *'like'* too much. Have a prize for the winner, too. This game helps prep your children for all of those school talks they have ahead of them.

KITCHEN ACTIVITIES

COLOURFUL KITCHEN VOLCANOES

What you'll need: An oven dish; several ramekins; baking soda; vinegar; food colouring; glitter.

1. Line a glass oven dish with around six ramekins and fill them three-quarters of the way with white vinegar. Let your child add a couple of drops of food colouring to each, preferably using lots of different colours.
2. Take a spoonful of baking soda, then drop it into one of the ramekins and watch the children' eyes widen.
3. Hand things over to your child and watch them go crazy setting off the other colourful volcanoes. Keep a stash of vinegar and baking soda handy so that you can refill the volcanoes when they're finished. Trust me, they'll be asking for more.

CREATE A CHALKBOARD WALL

What you'll need: Chalkboard paint; brushes or a roller; painter's tape; a moist cloth.

This is a great activity for the kitchen, as your children will have a place to be creative if you're busy cooking, working, or having a cuppa. It's a lovely activity to have the kids feel close to you while you're busy. Tip – when they inevitably get bored of this game, you can use the space yourself for reminders or recipes in future.

1 Start by picking out a wall, or part of a wall – it should be completely smooth and untextured. Wipe the wall down with a soft cloth to remove any dirt or dust.

2 Check whether your chalkboard paint needs a primer. If so, apply this first, otherwise you're ready to paint right away. Start by marking out the area to be painted with painter's tape; make sure it's at a height where your children can access it, too.

3 Once the area's marked up, use your brush or roller to apply strokes until you've covered the whole space. You can even hand a roller to your children – they'll love slapping paint all over the wall. You'll probably want to apply two to three coats, allowing for drying in-between. Keep some chalk in a little basket nearby and you're set.

DINOSAUR FOSSILS

What you'll need: A cup of used coffee grounds; half a cup of cold coffee; half a cup of salt; a cup of flour. (Cafes are often happy to supply used grounds – they're also great for your plants).

If you've got children that love playing with dinosaur toys, this activity should really be a hit with them.

1 Start by helping them mix together the coffee grounds, salt, cold coffee and flour in a mixing bowl. They will be wondering, *what sort of cake is this?*

2 Once you've got your thickened mixture, take out a handful and place it on some baking paper. Have them smash it flat using the heel of their hand, leaving a piece that's around half an inch thick. Keep going until you've got a full baking sheet or you run out of the mixture.

3 Now it's time for their dinosaur toys to get in on the action. Have them walk their dinosaurs across the mixture to create footprints. At this point, you can sprinkle in some bits of leaves from the garden. If you really want to get as authentic as possible and have any chicken bones leftover from a roast or takeaway, why not sprinkle those in too.

DINOSAUR FOSSILS *(continued)*

4 The final step is to pop the fossils into the oven for 30 minutes at 200 degrees. Once they're done, slide them off the cookie sheet and let them cool overnight. By morning, your children will have some awesome dinosaur fossils to accompany their prehistoric figures.

HOMEMADE PLAY DOUGH

What you'll need: 2 mixing bowls; a wooden spoon; 2 cups plain flour; ½ cup of salt; 1 ½ cups cream of tartar; 1 tbsp oil; 1 cup boiling water; 1 tsp vanilla or almond essence; gel food colouring (multiple colours).

1. In one mixing bowl, combine the water, oil, and vanilla or almond essence. In the other bowl, mix together all of the dry ingredients.
2. Add the liquid into the bowl containing the dry ingredients, then help your child beat them all together with the spoon until they've combined. As you would with bread, have your child knead the mixture into a dough; show them how to do it using your hands. Add either a few drops of water or a sprinkle of flour if it's cracking or too sticky.
3. Separate the dough into pieces – one for each colour of gel food colouring you have. This recipe should make around three separate colours. They love this bit – using the end of a teaspoon, dab a drop or two of each colour to separate pieces of dough.

HOMEMADE PLAY DOUGH *(continued)*

4 Finish by folding the colour into the dough and knead it again until you have an even colour throughout (you can add more gel if you want more vibrant colours).

If you have any essential oils around, pop a few drops in when mixing. My favourites for this are orange oil, peppermint, and lavender. Lavender is perfect if they need a little calming down, orange and peppermint are a lovely, fresh pick-me-up for flat moods.

INDOOR BUBBLES

What you'll need: Some plates; some paper straws (much better for the environment); dish soap.

1 Start with a plate and add a teaspoon of dish soap to a small amount of water.

2 Next, each takes a straw and dips the tip into the solution on the plate so that a thin layer of soap forms at the end.

3 Task them with seeing who can blow the biggest bubble by blowing gently into the straw. Make sure you remind them to blow *out,* not in! You could also challenge them to see who can blow their bubble furthest, or hold it on the end of their straw for the longest.

INVISIBLE INK EXPERIMENT

What you'll need: A thin paintbrush; some paper; any of these: acidic fruit juice; onion juice; vinegar; white wine; diluted honey; diluted cola; milk.

1 Start by preparing your 'ink'. The great thing is that you can use a whole range of products you'll probably have stashed away in your cupboard or fridge. Pour the ink of your choice into a small jar that can act as the 'inkwell' for your children to use.

2 Tell your children to get into 'super-spy' mode! Task them with communicating messages to each other without you (the parents) finding out. Or, if they share the technique with a friend (or you with their parents), they can write secret letters to each other by mail. Who doesn't love a secret?

3 When it's time to reveal the messages, all you need is a little warmth. If they are doing this themselves, holding the paper against a warm radiator is enough. You can also hold it up to a hot bulb, iron the paper, or put it in the oven below 200 degrees. Obviously, you'll need to be around for this part.

(continued on next page)

INVISIBLE INK EXPERIMENT *(continued)*

4 If you want to take this activity further, your children could try to see who can create the coolest designs on paper without being able to see them. Once they've finished, you can reveal the patterns and judge the winning picture.

5 While you can make even sneakier messages that can only be revealed with specific chemical reactions, these 'inks' are harder to come by, as well as more pungent or generally unpleasant for children to handle. Check out the appendix if you want to know more. A twist on this can be for them (perhaps littler ones) to draw or write on white paper with a white crayon. Use watercolor paints to reveal the pictures and messages.

MAGIC WAND BISCUITS

What you'll need: 100g butter; 85g icing sugar; 175g plain flour; 1 tsp vanilla extract; 1 tbsp milk; 1 egg yolk; cling film; wooden kebab skewers; a star-shaped cookie cutter; baking parchment. For the icing, you'll need 400g icing sugar; 3-4 tbsp water; 2-3 drops of several food colourings; cake toppings.

1 Start by preheating the oven to Gas mark 4 (180°C) while your child mixes together the butter, flour, and sugar. Get them to dive in with their hands and rub the mixture together with their fingers until it resembles bread-crumbs. Then, you're ready to mix the egg yolk, vanilla extract, and milk in. Once they've been combined, the mixture can be turned out onto your work surface.

2 Next show the cooks how to knead the mixture into a dough using their hands. Once the dough is a smooth, even consistency that isn't sticky, wrap it in cling film and put it into the fridge for 30 minutes. While it's chilling, help your child soak your kebab skewers in water. There's so much to learn in this activity especially if you explain the steps along the way – for example, why does the dough need to be popped into the fridge? Why do the skewers need to be soaked? Make sure you know the answers!

(continued on next page)

MAGIC WAND BISCUITS *(continued)*

3 Once the dough is chilled, roll it out onto a surface lightly dusted with flour so that the dough is around 1 cm thick. Hand your child the star cookie cutters and let them cut out as many star shapes as possible; you should get around 12 from these ingredients. Push a skewer into each of the stars to create the magic wands. Place each of them onto baking parchment and then bake them in the oven for around 15 minutes until they're golden brown. It's pretty exciting when they are brought out of the oven.

4 Now it's time to make the icing while the cookies cool down. Mix the icing sugar and water together in a bowl, leaving it runny but thick enough to spread without being too drippy. Here's where you can divide the sugar into several bowls and add different food colouring to each bowl.

5 All that's left to do is get creative with the wands. Once they've cooled enough to ice, things get messy. Let your child do whatever they like with the icing and the cake toppings, decorating their own wands. You can even use these as part of roleplay if your children have any witch, wizard or fairy outfits.

MAKE GLUE FROM MILK

What you'll need: ¼ cup hot water; ½ tsp baking soda; 1 tbsp vinegar; 2 tbsp powdered milk; water; coffee filters.

If you need PVA glue for an art project but don't have any, this makes a great replacement. Making glue from milk? You'll have to prove it for the children to believe you.

1 Supervise the mixing together of hot water (not boiling) with the milk powder. Keep stirring until all the lumps are gone. Then, pour in the tablespoon of vinegar and you'll see the milk begin to separate as the children stir.

2 Pour the mixture into your coffee filter, over a cup to capture the liquid. Make sure you keep what's captured in the filter. Squeeze this out to remove any excess moisture, then throw away the liquid and retain the contents of the coffee filter. Cut the solid mixture up into small pieces using a spoon or knife.

3 Now, add a tablespoon of hot water along with the baking soda to your solid mixture. You might get some foaming here due to the CO2 gas released by the chemical reaction, which should be fun for the children.

4 Stir your mixture again until it becomes smooth and more of a liquid, adding more water if it's too thick or more baking soda if it's too lumpy. Depending on the process and precision of ingredients, your children will be left with glue that's anywhere from a thick liquid to a paste. Best of all, it's non-toxic, so there's no need to call emergency if they stuff the brush into their mouth.

MAGNETIC SLIME

What you'll need: Liquid starch; PVA glue; iron oxide powder; a mixing bowl; something disposable for stirring; a measuring cup and spoon; a neodymium magnet (a regular one won't do – you'll have to buy this). (You might look at the iron oxide and battery and think 'where on earth do I get those?' Well, a certain large online retailer is a perfect place to start.)

This would not be a complete list if it did not include some sort of slime! The only problem with this activity is that the children will just be bursting for it to be ready *now*.

1 Pour ¼ cup of PVA glue into a mixing bowl and add two tablespoons of iron oxide powder. Give the mixture a thorough stir.

2 Add cup of liquid starch to the mixing bowl and let them stir it into the mixture. As the ingredients begin to combine, you'll see the mixture turning into a sort of slime.

3 At this point, you can begin kneading the mixture with your hands, like bread dough. It might need a brief rinse under the tap to wash away any excess starch.

MAGNETIC SLIME *(continued)*

4 Now, it's ready. Use the magnet to stretch, bend, and twist the slime around.

Warning – tie up long hair when dealing with slime – and your child's hair too. And just be careful with long beards.

Note: these are very strong magnets and should be handled individually to avoid fingers being pinched between more than one magnet. Additionally, handle the iron oxide with care and don't let your children do this part of the mixing while it's still in its powder form as the dust isn't great to inhale.

PIZZA FACES

What you'll need: Tomato sauce or passata; grated cheddar or mozzarella; sliced bread; pizza toppings (peppers, tomatoes, sweetcorn, ham, pineapple, pepperoni, olives).

These awesome pizza faces are a tasty alternative to sandwiches for lunch, as well as being much more fun to make.

1 Start by preparing your toppings; the ones I've listed above are the best for creating facial features on the pizzas. You can also toast your bread while this is going on. You can of course use dough, but toasting bread will still taste great and makes the activity prep so much easier. Who doesn't like easy!

2 Spread a thin layer of passata onto each piece of toast. This is a great task, like any that involves spreading some kind of sloppy mess onto a surface. Make sure it's covering each piece up to the edges.

3 Have all your toppings in bowls within easy reach. This is the part where they can sprinkle on the cheese and then create goofy characters using the toppings. Cooking the pizzas is as simple as putting them under the grill until the cheese has melted down. I guarantee that this time at least, all their meal will be eaten.

POTATO PRINTING

What you'll need: A potato; pencils; paper; a knife; acrylic paint; a paintbrush.

I remember doing this as a child – do you?

1 Cut a potato into thick slices – it's best that you handle this part. In the meantime, your child can sketch out a design for their potato stamp.

2 When the design is ready, centre the design over the middle of the potato flesh and score a line around the outline using a knife.

3 Carve away the potato around the outside of the scored line, to around 2-3cm in depth.

4 Pat the potato dry. Once the stamp is ready, it's time to get messy. Squeeze some acrylic paint onto a piece of cardboard or a paper plate. For a cleaner design, they can apply the paint to the stamp with a brush, or they can just dive right in with the stamp.

ROCK CANDY CRYSTALS

What you'll need: 3 cups of sugar; 1 cup of water; a pan; the microwave or hob; string; a pencil or knife; a glass jar; hard candies; food colouring.

1 Add the sugar and water to a pan and bring to the boil, letting the child carefully stir from time to time. You need to make sure the mixture boils, but you don't want to overdo it.

2 Keep stirring the solution until the sugar has been completely dissolved. Your mixture should turn clear, or the colour of straw. At this point add the food colouring so that the crystals will be more vibrant and exotic looking. If you use more than one pan, you can get different colours going. You can do it!

3 Decant the sugar into a container and place it in the fridge until it has cooled to slightly below room temperature. While it's cooling, get your child to help prepare your next step. Tie the string to a pencil or bread knife, or anything else that you can suspend over the jar.

4 Now, you need to 'seed' the string with sugar crystals to start the process off. Either dampen the string using the cooling mixture in the fridge, then dip it into raw sugar, or soak it for a while in the mixture.

ROCK CANDY CRYSTALS *(continued)*

5 The string needs to hang into the jar without touching the sides or the bottom. Since you need the string to stay firmly in place, ask your child to tie a hard candy to the bottom of the string, which will weigh it down. Double-check their handiwork to make sure that the candy won't slip off.

6 When your mixture is a little below room temperature, pour it into the glass jar. Have your child hang their strings suspended over the jar but touching the liquid, then place the jar somewhere it won't be disturbed.

7 While you can remove the crystals and eat them at any time (the children will be amazed at this), when you're happy with the size, leave them ideally for 3 to 7 days. But the kids will love to check on them from time to time. Just encourage them not to poke at or disturb them – in other words, tell them not to dive in when you're not looking!

OUTDOOR ACTIVITIES

If you're lucky to have a garden or patio, courtyard or balcony, there's plenty that your children can do even when you're stuck at home. Some of these activities only need take a few moments to set up, and then you can either join in or just leave them to it!

AUTUMN LEAVES

What you'll need: Lots of pretty autumn leaves; Mod Podge; white paint-pen; optional – string; holepunch.

My daughter and I love to display these. It really celebrates the colourful beauty of the season, and helps create memories made by collecting and playing in the leaves.

1. Collect the prettiest autumn leaves from your garden, neighbourhood or local park. Make sure you stop and have a good old play too while you're there! I still have memories of stomping in piles of crunchy leaves and throwing them into the air.

2. Lay the leaves out on newspaper to dry; you don't want any moisture left in them.

3. With a paintbrush, help your child coat the leaves in Mod Podge. They will love to watch them dry and see their colors deepen and become shiny. Once they have dried, make sure you flip them over (the leaves, not the kids) and do the other side. Once fully dried, pretty them up with painted stripes, dots or decoration of the crafter's own choosing.

4. Gently use a hole punch to make a little hole in each leaf, then thread through some string. Then your autumn garland is all ready to hang up in your home!

BUILD A BOTTLE ROCKET

What you'll need: Paper; duct tape; an empty 500ml soda bottle; thin cardboard; a ruler and pencil; some modelling clay or play dough; tap water; a cork; a bicycle pump.

1 Roll a piece of A4 paper into a cone, which will be your rocket's nose. Completely wrap the outside of the cone with duct tape.

2 Using more duct tape, attach the rocket's nose cone to the bottom of the soda bottle. Make sure it's well secured and pointing straight, just like NASA boffins would make.

3 Take your thin cardboard and help cut out three or four equally sized triangles that will be the fins for your rocket. Space them equally apart and low enough that the rocket can stand up, then affix them to the rocket. They will be jumping with excitement by this point.

4 Use play dough or modelling clay to wrap around the opening of the bottle, then wrap more duct tape around the clay to hold it in place. This will give the nose of the rocket more weight and stability.

(continued on next page)

BUILD A BOTTLE ROCKET *(continued)*

5 Make a small hole through the centre of your cork and check that it's the right size for the valve of your bicycle pump. Then, fill your bottle with tap water.

6 Stuff the cork into the bottle opening and make sure it's airtight. Then, push the end of the bicycle pump valve that's pointed into the hole you created in the cork. Again, ensure it's pushed tightly in.

7 Attach your bicycle pump tubing to the valve and then place the rocket facing upward outdoors. The rocket's going to shoot up fast, so please, keep your faces away from it. To launch the rocket, pump air into it using the bicycle pump. Once the pressure is high enough, the rocket will launch from the ground and propel water behind it. The children will love the science behind this – and they'll love getting wet. A *Super Parent* could combine this with bath day.

CREATE A BUG BOX

What you'll need: An open-fronted box; a small log; pine cones; small stones; twigs; dried grass; a drill.

This really is one of my favourite activities in this book – checking to see which new residents have moved into the home you built just for them.

1 Start by helping to gather a mix of natural materials from around the garden, or out on a park walk. A small log will provide a good centrepiece, and you can add pinecones, small rocks, twigs and dried grass. Just the collecting of pine cones and materials will be a fun activity.

2 If you've managed to find a good log, drill small holes through it, which will encourage lone bees and other insects to make a habitat inside of your bug box. Little bug homes!

3 Add some clumps of dried grass, a few pine cones, small stones and twigs to the box. This should attract other insects like ladybirds and woodlice, and you might even find a mouse or toad making a home inside.

4 Take your children out into the garden to check on the box every couple of days. You could create a 'mini-beasts manual' using the insects you find (see page 122).

CREATE A BEE HOTEL

What you'll need: Ceramic or terracotta plant pot; some modelling clay; string; bamboo canes or plastic straws; scissors or a hand saw.

1 Trim your bamboo canes or plastic straws so that they fit the depth of your plant pot. Scissors will of course tackle straws, but you might need a chef's knife or saw to cut through the bamboo.

2 Once the tubes are all cut to length, tie them together using your piece of string.

3 At the bottom of your plant pot, squidge the modelling clay in so that it's stuck firm and covers the base. Then squeeze down the bamboo/straws on it.

4 Find a quiet spot in your garden to place the pot and then wait until some beautiful buzzy bees move in. If you can, have it somewhere elevated from the ground for greater protection.

CREATE A SIMPLE TENT DEN

What you'll need: Some tarp or a sheet; rope or tough twine; tent pegs.

1 Run a length of rope or tough twine between two trees in the garden – you can do this in the woods, but it'll be a bother to take down every time you do it.

2 Lay the tarp or sheet across the taught twine towards one end of the material. Run some additional rope or twine from the overhanging segment of the tarp to the ground, creating the opening to the den.

3 Secure the longer section of tarp to the ground using tent pegs, so the play area is protected from the mud or grass.

4 Add blankets, toys, or even – wait for it – a mini-fridge filled with juice and healthy snacks. Or anything else to theme out the den and make it fun.

Things to do with your den ... ➥

DEN WARS

What you'll need: Nerf guns and nerf darts; targets or a collection of empty tin cans; all the cushions off the sofas.

1 Get your children to put together a sofa-cushion fort. If there's more than one child, have them do so at opposite ends of the room. If you've only one child, you can get involved and build your own fort – you'll love it. If you're doing this with an outdoor den, make it a little more robust with extra branches, leaves, or extra sheets.

2 Stack targets or a few towers of tin cans at various heights and positions around your forts; the more you have the better.

3 When both forts are built and targets set, have one gun and a stack of darts inside of each fort. Then the children – or yourself if you're taking part – can take turns in taking pot shots at each other's fort. The first to knock over all enemy targets is the indisputable winner!

CREATE A SENSORY DEN

What you'll need: Blackout fabric; clothes pegs; UV fabric; UV toys; glow sticks; UV light; UV paint, brushes and paper; marbles; electric fans; tissue paper; anything else you can think of.

Get creative with this one to create an experience they won't forget!

1 Start by creating a 'blackout den'. If you can get your hands on blackout fabric and some clothes pegs, then you should be able to create a close-fitting den that lets no light in. If you use some UV fabric with UV lights, this will make the whole thing even better.

2 Fill the den with a selection of toys and items that'll fit well with the sensory experience. The best kind of things to use include glow sticks, UV toys, electric fans (with guarded blades), hanging tissue paper, spy pens, and containers filled with marbles. You get the idea – anything that'll make for a great sensory experience that targets your children's sense of touch, sound, or hearing.

(continued on next page)

CREATE A SENSORY DEN *(continued)*

3 Wait until the sun sets and switch off the lights. Switch on any of the electrical gadgets inside your sensory den, including the UV lights, then let your children explore. You could provide UV paint, brushes, and paper as part of the activity, too. Or you could set up multiple dens with different kinds of experiences inside each of them – one with painting, another with as many kinds of funky lighting as you can find, and another with containers filled with different materials.

CREATE A READING DEN

What you'll need: Soft blankets; cushions; fairy lights; books.

1 Make their den as comfy and cosy as possible. Fill it with soft blankets to cover the floor, cushions from the sofa or bed – or even a duvet if you want to make it *really* tempting – and maybe even a few of their favourite soft toys. You want to make this a space that's as irresistibly comfortable as the child's own beds.

2 String fairy lights across the roof of the den. You want enough light that it's possible to read, while not having so much that it ruins the atmosphere. A couple of strings of white Christmas tree lights should do the trick.

3 Grab a few favourite books or invest in some new titles for the occasion. If you make the den large enough, you could even fit inside to read them their favourite story.

Another idea is to try out some diary writing. If you've lugged their duvets into the den you could read them a bedtime story and watch them fall asleep inside their temporary bedroom – they will ask to sleep in there anyway, I know it. Just don't serve them breakfast in it or you'll never get them out.

CREATE A BEACH-THEMED DEN

What you'll need: Waterproof plastic or fabric; a bag of sand; sand moulds; buckets; spades; swimming costumes.

1 Wherever you live you can bring the beach to your home with this cool beach-themed den idea. Start by building your den, preferably inside a conservatory or enclosed patio to make the clean-up operation easier when you're finished; sand, as we all know, can live in all sorts of clothing and body nooks for months.

2 Lay down some waterproof fabric or plastic on the ground – again, this will make the clean-up task easier later. Tip a bag of sand across the ground inside the den until you can no longer see any fabric or flooring. Sand is pretty easily and cheaply available in large DIY stores, and even toy shops.

3 Bring in a hoard of beach toys: buckets, spades, balls, sand moulds, beach towels, and anything else that you can think of. You could also make a packed lunch with juice boxes, just like you would on a trip to the seaside. If you're feeling brave, cart in a bucket of water, too; this will let your children make sandcastles if you mix a little with the sand from the den.

EGG CARTON GARDEN

What you'll need: An egg carton; some dirt; seeds of your choice; thin card.

1 Decide what you're going to plant – you might want to do this ahead of time, as you'll need to get some seeds before you get started. Make an outing of choosing some seeds to get them interested in the project. Cut out some small rectangular name cards (or lolly sticks) with a pointed end that you can stick into the dirt.

2 Cut the lid off your egg carton, exposing all the grooves which are where you'll grow your seeds. While you do this, your children can write the names of the seeds you'll be growing on the name cards.

3 Fill each of the grooves with dirt. While you can use dirt from the garden, you'd have more success using organic dirt for anything you're planning to harvest and eat.

4 Let your children make a small hole in the soil with their finger, pop the seed in and carefully cover it with a light layer of soil. Water each of the containers lightly, but be careful not to saturate and soak the cardboard.

(continued on next page)

EGG CARTON GARDEN *(continued)*

5 Leave your new mini-garden on a sunny windowsill and have your child water them regularly, keeping the soil moist but not soaking. A cute little watering can could go a long way to encourage them to look after their seedlings. When you see the shoots sprout up, you might notice them rotating towards the sun, so turn the carton from time to time.

6 Once your plants have outgrown their cartons, you can either transplant them outside or into a larger pot. If you're growing herbs to use for cooking, you can involve them in gathering some for dinner, scatter some on pizzas, on top of omelettes, whatever you like.

GARDEN TREASURE HUNT

What you'll need: A checkbox list of items to find; a clipboard; a pencil; some 'treasure'.

This a great activity for when children have friends over. It burns off some initial excitement, and if they like, they can draw their specimens too.

1 Create a list of items for the children to find. You could either have this be a checklist on a piece of paper, or give them a single clue that leads them to the next written clue that's hidden somewhere in the garden. Some ideas can be a smooth stone, spider web, feather, piece of bark, pretty leaf, flower, moss, etc.

2 Attach the lists to clipboards and give one to each of your children with a pencil or crayon.

3 See how long it takes for them to solve the treasure hunt. You could hide the 'treasure' at the end of the final clue, or if you're *super-parenting* and going down the educational route, have it as a prize for the first person to complete their list.

GARDEN WATER PARK

What you'll need: Outdoor paddling pool; hosepipe and sprinklers; water balloons; water pistols; heavy-duty plastic sheeting; liquid soap; tent pegs.

1. Fill up the paddling pool on a warm day. Children love splashing around outside, but we're going to take outdoor water fun to a new level.
2. Lay a long sheet of heavy-duty plastic down in the garden – preferably on a shallow incline. Smooth the sheet over with your hands and pin the sides down with tent pegs.
3. Cover the centre of the slide with a thin layer of liquid soap; this will help make it hilariously slippery. Then, spray the whole thing over with a hose to create a long slip and slide.
4. Fill up a few dozen water balloons and toss them into a container left by the side of the garden. Fill up any water guns if you have them and space them out around the garden. Get ready for the happy squeals.
5. If you have sprinklers, set them up at different areas of the garden on a rotation or spraying in one direction, creating a wall of water to run through.

GARDEN WATER PARK *(continued)*

6 Now you've made their very own outdoor water park that'll not only keep them busy for hours, but also cool and happy. You could even take this further and position a garden slide to drop them directly into the paddling pool, using the same liquid soap and water idea. Leave a hose trickling at the top of the slide to make it more fun.

MAKE A CAKE FOR BIRDS

What you'll need: 85g lard or suet; some wild bird seed; a handful of peanuts; a handful of raisins; grated cheese; a mixing bowl and wooden spoon; some empty yoghurt pots with holes punched through the bottom.

1 A cake for a bird? The children will be intrigued. Before you start, take your lard or suet out of the fridge and let it warm to room temperature so that it's softened and easier to work with.

2 Add the rest of your ingredients to your mixing bowl, and let them mix it up. Mmm, does it look delicious?

3 Cut the lard or suet into smaller pieces and gradually mix them in.

4 Take your string and double it over, then tie a knot at the end. Thread the string through the hole in the bottom of a yoghurt pot so that the loop you've created is hanging above the pot and the knot holds it in place.

5 Add some of your mixture to the yogurt pots and then stick them into the fridge until they set. Once they've hardened remove the outer pots. If you have the muscle, hoist your children up to some low-hanging tree branches so that they can be hung for the birds. Now put on your bird-watcher hats and watch your feathered friends visit for a snack.

MAKE A KITE

What you'll need: Paper (around 8.5x11-inches); a wooden kebab skewer or plastic drinking straw; string; some ribbon; scissors; sticky tape.

Because making a kite is part of every childhood...

1 The first step is to fold that piece of paper in half horizontally, before marking a point along the top of the paper, around an inch from the fold, then marking another dot on the bottom-right corner of the paper, again around an inch from the fold. Don't worry if you're winging it – if it's not precisely even, it won't matter too much. Now draw a line that connects the dots diagonally.

2 Fold one side of the paper along the diagonal line you've just drawn, then flip the whole thing over and fold the other side down to match. Once you've created your folds, fold the flap back to its original position, then flip the paper back over to its original side.

3 You should now have just one of the flaps folded over and pointing to the left. Tape all the way along the seam (the fold), then lie a skewer or straw along the top of the kite shape, from point to point. Cut it down

(continued on next page)

to size so that it doesn't protrude beyond the edges of the kite, then tape it into place.

4 Flip the kite onto its front, so that the skewer is face down, then straighten out the 'spine' of the kite.

5 Mark another spot around a third of the way down the back of the kite, approximately an inch away from the edge, then tape over the spot to strengthen it. Use your scissors to punch a hole through the spot.

6 Hand your children the spool of string and have them thread the string through the hole you've just created, then tie it tightly – but not so tight that it tears the kite. Then tape a length of ribbon to the bottom point of the kite to trail behind it in the wind.

7 All you need now is a windy day, and sadly you can't buy these on Amazon. If you struggle to get the kite off the ground, consider swapping out a skewer for a straw (plastic is lighter), or using less ribbon (or more lightweight ribbon overall). Let them know from the start that adjustments may need to be made, and it's all part of the building and designing experience.

MAKE A MINI-BEAST MANUAL

What you'll need: Some paper or thin card; pens and pencils; colouring pencils; a stapler; a printer (optional: a polaroid camera, magnifying glass, binoculars); glue.

1 Explore the garden with your little one(s) on a hunt for wildlife. Check the trees for birds, gently overturn rocks for creepy crawlies, and check the bushes for other insects such as butterflies and ladybirds. Ants are great fun to watch. You'll be surprised how much life is there right outside your door. Get the children to take a picture of any they find on a smartphone or camera (or polaroid camera if you have one), or draw them in a little notebook, like real explorers do.

2 Send the pictures to your computer and then print them all out. Then help the budding zoologists search for each of the animals or insects online, and find out some facts about each of them.

3 Create a miniature booklet out of folded A4 paper or thin card, stapled down the spine. On each page, they can stick down one of the pictures on one side of the booklet, then write a few facts out about each one on the other side of the page. This can be simple things for younger age groups, like the animal's name, its usual colours, its habitat, and so on.

NATURE MANDALA

What you'll need: Just a yard; park or forest.

1 Choose a lovely day and head out into nature with the children to collect a variety of natural items such as flowers, twigs, leaves of different shapes, colours and sizes and patterns, bark, grasses, stones, pebbles, seeds, pine cones.

2 Help your child arrange the items starting from the middle and working their out, creating rings each time. Play around with different styles and patterns – for example leaves in a circle, leaves pointing straight out, pebbles scattered at even points; petals can be sprinkled in certain areas.

3 When they've finished their natural masterpiece, don't forget to take a picture so it can be remembered forever.

NATURE MOBILE

What you'll need: A selection of flowers, twigs, and leaves; a ball of string; scissors; coloured wool or string; an embroidery hoop.

1 Take your children out into the garden to gather the materials you'll need. Leaves, twigs, and flowers of varying colours and sizes will produce the best results.

2 Have them gather the leaves and flowers together and tie them at intervals on lengths of string. The string should be cut to various lengths, so the items on the mobile don't all hang at the same height.

3 Tie the smaller twigs you've gathered together into squares, triangles and crosses using coloured wool. Create some more lengths of string and tie your finished twigs to them, again at various lengths.

4 Fasten all your hanging pieces onto the embroidery hoop. If you want to pretty it up even more, you can loop lengths of coloured string from one side of the hoop to the other or wind it around the full circle. These also make beautiful natural gifts for family and friends.

Or hang it in your child's room to bring the outdoors in.

NATURE'S PAPER

What you'll need: Different coloured pieces of sugar paper; some sharpies.

1 Start by writing down some grammatical terms on the pieces of paper – one for each piece. One could have 'verb' written on it, another could be 'noun', another 'adjective', and so on.

2 Lay the pieces of paper down on a patio or chair in the garden, weighed down by a rock. Then explain the plan. They must collect items that can fit into each of the categories. For example 'a red leaf' – then they'd write the word 'red' on the leaf and place it on the 'adjective' pile. Or they could collect a twig for the 'noun' card.

3 Wait till they've filled up the various cards then go through their finds with them. You could use the bits and pieces they've collected to do another activity, such as the nature mandala, mobile or nature picture on pages 124-127.

NATURE'S PAPER *(continued)*

4 You can adapt the same idea for developing other skills. You could write single or double-digit numbers onto leaves and use them for addition and subtraction, multiplication, and division exercises. For a longer activity, they could stencil designs onto leaves with a sharpie, and then fill them in with paints to create story flashcards.

NATURE PICTURE

What you'll need: String; scissors; double-sided sticky tape; a thick sheet of cardboard; a strong stick, longer than the cardboard's width; some leaves, flowers, twigs, or feathers.

1 Grab a container and head into the garden with the children. Hunt down your materials, including twigs, flowers, leaves, and anything else they want to add to the finished picture.

   There are no rules! Try to find a long enough twig to act as the backing frame for your picture, too.

2 Get them to completely cover the cardboard backing with strips of your double-sided sticky tape. Then peel off the back of the tape and you're ready to start.

3 Help arrange all of the natural materials into a pattern. You could use a pencil to lightly sketch some guide outlines – for example, a forest or flower picture. Then they can fix the materials in place.

4 When the picture's done, attach further strips of tape to the back of the cardboard sheet along the top. Peel the backing away and press the twig into place on the back of the picture.

NATURE PICTURE *(continued)*

5 Finish by tying a length of string to each side of the twig, which should protrude from the corners of the cardboard 'frame'. Now you can hang it – outside or inside.

NATURE SHOP

What you'll need: An outdoor space; a collection of natural materials, including branches and twigs; pinecones; pine needles; leaves; small rocks – whatever your children can find.

The beauty of this shop is that it can open during a pandemic without breaching safety guidelines!

1 Tell your children that they're going to create their very own outdoor nature shop; all children love to play shops. Find a space that's appropriate for it. My daughter loved this idea and one day in the woods, we came across a covered over space where some trees had fallen. This was the perfect location for the shopfront.

2 Next stock up the shop. My daughter found all kinds of foods to sell at her store – twigs became chips, pine needles became green beans, and assorted leaves made the perfect lettuce. There are so many other items you could use, including larger stones and smaller pebbles, flower petals, tree bark, acorns and conkers, and so on.

NATURE SHOP *(continued)*

3 Your children should also work out what to use as currency. For us, this was smaller pebbles and pine cones. Then they can take on the role of the store owner and you – or your other children – can be the customers. They'll have a lot of fun with this, while you can feel accomplished in that they'll be practising valuable social skills and numeracy without even realising it. *Super Parent* strikes again!

OUTDOOR GOLF COURSE

What you'll need: Large red cups; some kid-sized golf clubs (improvise if you don't have any); clipboard and paper; a pencil or pen.

1 Mark out a golf course on your lawn. Get creative; use large red cups on their side as the holes, or other household cups will do if you have none. You could use large branches or rocks to mark out the edges of each fairway or as guidance to follow around the course.

2 Hand each of your children (players) a golf club, and a clipboard and paper. If you're not playing, you could be the scorekeeper. Keep a tally of the number of shots it takes for each player to complete the holes around the course. Who knows, you may have just inspired a love of golf.

PARACHUTING TOYS

What you'll need: Scissors; thin fabric (like a handkerchief); strong twine; some toys, like action figures or Stunt Barbie.

1 Take your thin fabric and cut out a square around 20cm by 20cm (larger if it's a heavy or bulky toy). You could use a heavy-duty carrier bag if you don't have fabric; this is what I did often as a child, as there never seems to be a shortage of carrier bags in the house.

2 Using the scissors, make small slits in each corner of the material, not too close to the corner to minimise the risk of tearing.

3 Attach a length of twine (around 15 to 20cm) to each corner. You could use string, though the increased weight could make the toy fall faster and cut the fun short. And Barbie wouldn't be too pleased.

4 Tie the other end of each of the four pieces of twine to the toy. For example, with an action figure, you could tie all four lengths of twine to the character's head or neck. Don't worry, they're toys and don't feel pain.

5 They can now take their favourite toys out into the garden and enjoy tossing them up into the air then watching them parachute back to Earth. If it's raining, you could also drop them from the top of a high staircase.

TIME CAPSULE

What you'll need: Empty two-litre soda bottle; paper and scissors; a pen or colouring pens; a trowel; anything you want to store in your time capsule.

Are you excited for this? I'm still waiting for my old school to dig theirs up so I can get my catapult back. You're playing the long game with this one, of course; in years to come – or however often you like – the children can dig up the capsule and look back on the contents, updating or adding to the items inside.

1. Remove the old label from your empty soda bottle and clean away any sticky glue residue.
2. Give the children some paper and either have them write down some full sentences, or prepare the sentences beforehand, leaving gaps to be completed. For example, *"This year I learned how to ..."*, *"Some things that make me happy right now are ..."* or *"In the next 5 years, I want to achieve ..."*. They will prove to be extra cute when you read them in the future. My daughter included a wish that one day our two cats would become better friends (they don't get along too well right now).

TIME CAPSULE *(continued)*

3 Fill the bottle with a meaningful collection of other small objects they want to bury (like those sprouts you keep making them eat), and things they are sure to remember. This could be a family photo, a favourite toy they're willing to part with, or even a tape measure with a sheet of paper measuring each child's height. How about some handprints?

4 Find a good spot in the garden and get the children to dig a hole with the trowel, ensuring it's deep enough to cover the bottle plus a few additional inches to account for weather and soil shifting.

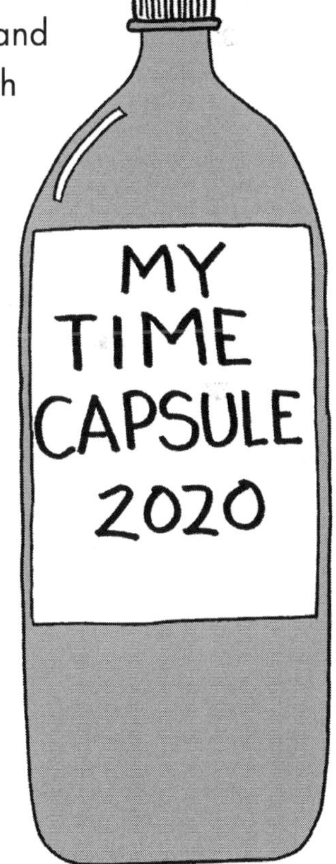

SCENARIOS AND ROLE-PLAYS

Children love role-play! I'll be honest with you – I can play games, get stuck into crafting, outdoor activities, you name it – but when it comes to role-play, I struggle.

If you feel the same perhaps get another family member involved, make the most of role-play activities when friends are over, or even try role-playing games through video chat (my daughter manages to have a wonderful time cooking up a pretend feast for her Nana on the other side of the world).

AD-HOC THEATRE

What you'll need: A pen; a small container; small pieces of paper; various dress-up outfits; props (hats, shoes, boots, sunglasses); juggling balls; bean bags; sports equipment; popcorn.

This is a bit like charades but with a real stage, lights and theatre atmosphere, which should bring out the performer in your child... not that many children need encouragement for that.

1 Ladies and gentleman, set up your stage area!

You can line up the dining room chairs facing the windows, with the curtains tied back to create the appearance of a stage and its audience. Use spotlighting if you can, focusing lamps on the performance area, or turn your lights to a dimmer shade of blue or red using an automated home assistant to create more of an atmosphere.

2 Think up a range of fun prompts to throw together an ad-hoc play. It could be a sport, activity, job, or even a circus, fairytale or real-life scenario they are re-enacting. Fold the pieces of paper, toss them into the container and mix them around.

3 Have the children come up and pick a prompt out of the container, then give them a minute to come up with a routine. After that, they'll have to perform it to you, their very own audience. You could even arrange a fun family/friend night so you'll have a bit more of a crowd to cheer and more little thespians to entertain you. Make sure someone films it on their phone or camera and watch it later together as a family.

BANK ROLE-PLAY

What you'll need: A pile of coins (and banknotes if you have them); thin card; pens; any leftover currency you've got lying around – Monopoly money if you've gone cashless.

1. Decide who's going to be who in your bank role-play. Ideally, you'll want your children to be customers, but they can switch roles throughout the activity. Somebody should man the cashier counter, and somebody should be on another desk for travel money. They love playing with money.

2. Hand out some money using your coins and banknotes. Hand any travel money you've got to the person playing the role of travel money cashier.

3. Decide what games you're going to incorporate into your pretend bank. You could have your children come to exchange their money into travel money, teaching them valuable skills about how foreign currency works in addition to basic calculations. But no bank robbers – crime does not pay!

EASY SUPERHERO MASKS

What you'll need: Different coloured felts; scissors; ribbon, elastic or string.

1. Ask the children if there are any particular superheroes they want to become, then fold a piece of coloured felt in half and cut out the shape for a mask. Once unfolded, the shape is a little like two stretched hexagons joined together.
2. Next fold each individual side to cut an eye hole along the fold.
3. Cut small slits at either end of the mask, then loop the elastic, ribbon or string and tie it off in a knot. Creating these masks only takes around five minutes and will give them a lot of superhero scenarios that they can role-play – either as the goodies or the baddies..

HOME RESTAURANT

What you'll need: A4 paper or thin card; cutlery and tableware; dining table; ingredients for a meal (three courses if you want to go all-out).

Making the menus was my daughter's favourite part of this activity; keep these menus to help preserve the memories!

1 As Head Chef, you'll need to tell your Restaurant Manager what possibilities there are for your menu – after all, you'll only have specific ingredients in the house. But if you want to be truly devious, you can throw in some wild cards; dishes that you don't have the ingredients for: *'Sorry sir, frog legs are off today.'*

2 Your child can get to work creating a menu on paper or card, which lists the dishes that the customers can choose from. They'll use the recommendations of what's available based on what the Head Chef has told them they can serve.

3 Have other family members or your spouse greeted at the door to the dining area. Your children can take their coats, seat them, and bring them their menus; tip them some pocket money, if you're feeling generous, for that authentic experience. If you've more than one

child, have one create the food menu while another does the drinks list.

4 Once your 'guests' have had time to peruse the options, they can order their drinks and their food selections from the friendly waiting staff. Of course, they're going to need some help preparing the food in the kitchen and serving hot dishes, but you can have a lot of fun with this if you go all-out on the activity and theming.

Make sure the guests dress up too, put some restaurant-style music on, and make a night of it. *Bon Appetit!*

INDOOR CAMPING

What you'll need: A tent that'll fit if pitched indoors; sleeping bags; food supplies like sausages and marshmallows; kebab skewers; a portable camping stove; drinking flasks.

It's time to take the shrink-wrap off that 'Field and Forest Sound Effects' CD you got for Christmas.

1 Clear out some space in the lounge or a conservatory to make space for the tent. Make it cosy. The children will have enough fun just running in and out of the tent, but you can go a little way to make it extra special.

   This kind of activity is great for something like a conservatory as it means you'll be able to safely use a camping stove to cook with.

2 If you've got smart assistant lights, you can dim the lighting to a very low level, perhaps in a red or orange colour to simulate dusk. Alternatively, if you've got an old projector that illuminates the room with stars, this is a great way to simulate the outdoor night sky. Another option is glow stickers; they're always fun.

INDOOR CAMPING *(continued)*

3 If you can set up the camping stove, or you have a real wood fireplace, you can help the children can cook some basic food over the flames. If you'd rather play it safe, you could ditch the food and just roast marshmallows on kebab skewers, or make smores in the oven.

4 Think of some fun camping-inspired activities to play with your children. Tell 'campfire' stories or sing songs – if you're a guitar player, this is the perfect time to break out the music.

LEARN DANCE MOVES

What you'll need: The TV (or YouTube); some old clothes or other props (sunglasses, hats, shoes).

1 You can use music channels for this if there are child-friendly ones available. If not, you could also set up YouTube on a laptop or cast it to your TV with a Chromecast, using a child-friendly playlist you've set up yourself.

2 Get your children to choose a music video, or select that one they've been playing seven-hundred and fifty times over the past week, and ask them if they want to learn the dance moves. Be brave and put on a performance for the family. Of course, they'll say yes.

3 Give them any props you can find around the house. Old clothes, hats, shoes, sunglasses – things like that. Those photo booths-for-hire that you see at weddings have prop kits that you can find yourself on websites like Amazon, and they've got a range of cool props inside. Pound shops will have lots of this kind of thing too.

LEARN DANCE MOVES *(continued)*

4 After they've had an hour or so of practice, get them to give you and the family their best performance. If they're willing, you could select another music video afterward, too. And don't forget to film it!

LEARN TO CODE THROUGH A GAME

Learning software development skills is now such a huge field that they've begun teaching it in school – if only I'd had that benefit as a child. I know, I know; dropping your children in front of a computer for education purposes will likely be met with confusion or yawns. But if your child is getting older, this game called 'Code Combat' will let them play a game that's super-entertaining while gradually teaching them basic coding skills. You'll feel pretty good about it too.

What you'll need: A computer.

1 Create an account at Code Combat and let the children pick their avatar.

2 The rest is simple. The game takes you through levels that increase in difficulty, but all the coding is in the context of moving your cute avatar around a dungeon and defeating baddies. It will be so much fun they won't know they are learning – perfect, what better way to learn.

MOVIE NIGHT

What you'll need: Duvets; a selection of movies; popcorn; fizzy sodas; sweets/chocolate; the TV.

1. While we all fall into the trap of plonking ourselves in front of the TV each night, it's a great way to wind down – but it can feel old very quickly if you get into a routine. So dedicate *one* night as official movie night to start the tradition off. You could choose a certain date each month or even do it once a fortnight or once a week. And it's something fun and comforting the children can look forward to.
2. Ask the children what movie they'd like to watch. To avoid the inevitable arguments it might be an idea to have them create a programme guide as an additional activity, and create a movie pamphlet for the film they decide on.
3. Make the night feel completely different – you don't want this to be a typical night in front of the TV. Drag the duvets off the beds and into the lounge. Make mountains of popcorn and serve cheese melted over nachos for dinner – eaten in front of the TV of course. If you've got smart lights, set the ambiance in different rooms to different colours and levels of brightness. Create the effect of a movie theatre so the children feel like they've been transported elsewhere. Beautiful memories made so easily!

PRETEND GROCERY STORE

What you'll need: A range of coins; some fake or real banknotes, or Monopoly money; fruits and vegetables (or toy ones); a variety of food boxes and tins; a toy shopping trolley if you have one.

Shopping is a very popular activity – I've lost count of the times we've played pretend grocer, or toy shop, or dress shop, wizard supply emporium etc.

1. Start by gathering some money together. If you have games with fake bank coins and notes, raid those. You could also create some notes from small pieces of paper, or just use real money if you're sure your children won't rip, ruin or lose it. My daughter also uses a pretend credit card (or one of my old ones) and loves to scan it when she pays.
2. On top of an upside-down box or other impromptu shop counter, lay out a selection of fruits and vegetables. Make little price tags too.

PRETEND GROCERY STORE *(continued)*

3 Take some empty – or full if needs be – tins, jars, and food boxes from the cupboards and let them set up another area near the fruit and vegetables. Just be careful, because the last thing we want is a full can falling on little toes. For my daughter, setting up was definitely the best part. (And definitely enough time for you to sit back and enjoy a coffee until the game begins).

4 Now, your children are ready to do some shopping. They'll love playing with the money – especially if they can use the real thing – and you can use it for educational purposes, too.

SHOEBOX PUPPET THEATRE

What you'll need: A shoebox; wrapping paper; scissors; a craft knife; tape; confetti; a length of fabric or tissue paper; finger puppets; small fairy lights.

1. Remove the lid from the shoebox and then cut out the bottom so that you're left with only the sides, and can fit your arm through the middle.
2. Turn the lid of the shoebox upside down and cut off one flap from one of the sides. At this point, if your box isn't a consistent colour, you can spray the whole thing black or cover it all in black sugar paper, gluing it down.
3. Lay your box lid down and then stand the square piece of the box on its side inside the lid, pressed up against the side with the remaining flap. You should see a stage area coming together now.
4. Cut out a piece of your wrapping paper so that it's a little larger than the surface area of the box lid. Fold the edges of the paper under so that it fits inside the lid area; the folds will keep the edges neat and the pretty wrapping paper design will liven up the stage. If there's a theme your child might love, go with that. It could be ballet, comedy, circus, farmyard – anything.

SHOEBOX PUPPET THEATRE *(continued)*

5 Using tape, secure a string of fairy lights along the top of the stage. It will look *adorable*.

6 With either tissue paper or fabric, create some curtains at each side of the stage and you've got your finished finger puppet theatre. Check out the pipe cleaner finger puppets on page 37 if you need some props.

SHOOT A STOP-MOTION MOVIE

What you'll need: Toys and other props you want to use; an iPhone; the Stop Motion Studio app.

Don't be surprised if they have this category at the Academy Awards one day!

1 Download the 'Stop Motion Studio' app onto an iPhone. If you have an Android or other phone, see what's available on your app store.

2 Break down a fun scene you're trying to shoot into frames and then work your way through the idea, positioning the toys frame-by-frame and capturing a picture of the scene at each stage. When you get into the app, you'll put them all together. Your children can help you position the toys and come up with the storyline. They could even write a clear script and one could be the director.

3 Use the app on your phone to string all the frames together and then test out the movie from start to finish. If you pull it off well, you'll have an animated movie featuring their favourite toys. Don't forget to keep it for posterity.

SHOOT A STOP-MOTION MOVIE *(continued)*

VIRTUAL HOLIDAY

If you can't take your children on holiday right now, why not bring the holiday to them? There's a lot you can do with this, like making your own passports and boarding cards, simulating a hotel check-in, and creating locally-inspired dishes (see the 'home restaurant' activity above). As an overall activity this can last for hours, depending on how far you go with it.

What you'll need: Thin card and paper; pencils, pens and colouring pencils; a hole puncher; Monopoly money; holiday clothes; a suitcase.

1 Start by having your children create their own passports. Fold over a thin piece of card into a booklet and see if you've any spare passport-sized photos left over from the last time you renewed their passports; they can always draw themselves in if you don't have any photos. Stick these into place on one side of the inner pages

2 Next fill out the rest of the passport information and cut out two rectangular pieces of thin card. Punch a series of spaced holes down one side of the card, a few centimetres from the edge, so that it can easily be torn away like a ticket stub when needed. Have them decide where they want to visit and then fill out the details of the flight on the boarding cards.

3 Depending on how far you want to take this, you could set out the chairs in the lounge in the

arrangement of a plane cabin (my daughter's favoured role in this play is 'Chief Flight Attendant').

As a special treat, perhaps little airplane activity packs could be handed out (isn't that the best part?)

Have somebody checking passports, validating tickets, and tearing off stubs at boarding. Pack a suitcase with holiday clothes and bring them onto the plane.

4 On 'arrival', you can simulate hotel check-in too. You could create bookings using paper or card and have somebody on reception to check all the details. If you've got a paddling pool – or even a swimming pool – then you could set up props in the garden to create a hotel scene.

5 For any activities you want to include, you can give each of your children some 'travel money' to spend. Start them off with some real currency and have them come to exchange their money as part of the activity; then, assign them some Monopoly money in exchange for their currency in the same way you'd exchange your travel money before flying. *Bon Voyage!*

MINIATURE HOUSES

What you'll need: Shoe boxes or cardboard boxes; thin card; paper; colouring pens; paints and brushes; glue; sticky tape.

1 Help your children to come up with an idea for what they can build first. For my daughter, this was a replica of Mr McGregor's garden from the 'Peter Rabbit' books. We started with a shoebox, adding a door and windows with paint. Then, we started the garden by adding raised vegetable beds, a washing line (think string and cocktail sticks), wooden fences made from lollipop sticks, and so on. Your children need an idea that has 'growth potential' – perhaps a recreation of their bedroom in miniature form, which could then grow outwardly to include the whole house.

2 Raid the recycling bin and crafting box. The great thing about this activity is that you can use anything, from empty bottles to tin cans, to cardboard and cocktail sticks. Make sure they have a whole pile of materials to work with, to stimulate creativity.

MINIATURE HOUSES *(continued)*

3 Once the architects have finished building their first masterpiece, they can talk you through what they've come up with. You can return to this time and time again. With my daughter, we worked on expanding that little garden every evening for around a week to develop it further. Once they're fully engrossed in the building, you can shut down the TV and the video games and look forward to a quiet, peaceful house, knowing your children are happily distracted in an absorbing activity.

INDEX

RESOURCES

HOMESCHOOLING ACTIVITIES & GUIDANCE

I've included the following home-schooling resource providers not only because they all provide such wonderful hands-on activity ideas to connect with your children and make learning fun, but also because of the support, guidance and inspiration they offer.

www.homeschoolden.co.uk
This site is run by Liesl. She provides lots of resources & printables including the **Ultimate Hands-On Homeschooling Guide** to Make Learning Exciting, Engaging and Memorable!

www.homeschoolcreations.net
On Jolanthe's site you will find free prinatables, helpful tips and resources as well as a free homeschool planner to help you get organised.

www.simplehomeschool.net
Jamie runs this site and along with a mountain of free creative resources she is also offering a **free** digital copy of her book called ***Secrets of a Successful Homeschool Mom***.

www.rockyourhomeschool.net
With an emphasis on self-care, Amy's website includes a library full of encouragement & free resources to help you connect with your kids... and stay relaxed while doing so!

CRAFT SUPPLIERS

United Kingdom (with worldwide online ordering)

Hobby Craft

www.hobbycraft.co.uk

Starting more than 25 years ago in 1994, Hobby Craft is now the largest arts and crafts retailer in the UK. As well as supplying materials for just about every crafting activity you could think of – including art, crochet, haberdashery, papercraft, baking, jewellery making, clay modelling and much more besides.

Hobby Craft also provide more than 1,500 easy-to-follow tutorials on a huge variety of crafting techniques and have a very active, free membership – the Hobby Craft Club. Members receive exclusive offers, ideas & guidance in special techniques.

United States & Canada (with worldwide online ordering)

A Cherry on Top

www.acherryontop.com

A Cherry On Top Crafts began in a little shoe box full of stickers more than 20 years ago and now carries thousands upon thousands of products including paper crafts, general crafts, needle arts, sewing & quilting supplies, art supplies, and so much more.

Their site features a gallery where you can share your projects and ideas and you can also join their crafty community and learn new techniques by chatting on their message boards or signing up for their free newsletter.

Exclusive Reader-only discount...
Get 10% off when you use this code: 'RPTEN'

YOURS FREE:

Don't forget your FREE 'Kid's Games' mini-guides as a thank you for buying this book.

'10 Fun Travel Games to Play with Your Kids'
'10 Fun Garden Games to Play with Your Kids'

If you haven't already done so, just visit the following page on my website and you'll be able to download them immediately:

GO HERE RIGHT NOW TO GET YOUR FREE COPIES:

www.liferaftmedia.com/10fun

Review request

I hope you and your child/children have a wonderful time together trying out some of the activities in this book. If you've enjoyed reading it and feel inspired by the ideas, please leave me a review on Amazon as your feedback is most appreciated.

To leave a review all you need to do is look the book up by title on Amazon. Once you're on the book's Amazon page, simply scroll down until you see the little button which says 'Write a customer review'. Click on that and you're good to go.

Have fun and thanks for your support.

Rob Plevin

What People Say About Rob Plevin's Teaching & Parenting Resources

"Thank you for helping us help our daughter."

The coaching Rob gave us was priceless. In just one session we were able to understand our daughter's needs and create an environment in which she could trust us. She came back on side almost straight away and we have all been getting on much better. We can now talk about her college placement without the arguments and flare ups of the past. Thank you for helping us help our daughter."

S. CARR

"... your strategies work wonders!"

"Thank you so much Rob for what you are doing for the profession, your strategies work wonders! I have never tried the 'pen' but will do next time! Seriously speaking, I give the link to your productions to many young teachers I know because they are so unhappy sometimes and they need help which they find with what you do! So, thanks again and carry on with your good job!"

MARIE ('TAKE CONTROL OF THE NOISY CLASS' CUSTOMER)

"We will be inviting Rob back on every possible occasion to work with all of our participants and trainees."

"We were delighted to be able to get Rob Plevin in to work with our Teach First participants. From the start his dynamic approach captivated the group and they were enthralled throughout. Rob covered crucial issues relating to behaviour management thoroughly and worked wonders in addressing the participants' concerns about teaching in some of the most challenging schools in the country. We will be inviting Rob back on every possible occasion to work with all of our participants and trainees."

TERRY HUDSON (REGIONAL DIRECTOR 'TEACH FIRST', SHEFFIELD HALLAM UNIVERSITY)

"Fantastic way to create a calm and secure learning environment for all the students." "Thanks so much, Rob. Fantastic way to create a calm and secure learning environment for all the students. It's great how you model the way we should interact with the students – firmly but always with respect."

MARION ('TAKE CONTROL OF THE NOISY CLASS' CUSTOMER)

"I will be recommending that the teachers in training that I deal with should have a look at these videos." "These tips and hints are put in a really clear, accessible fashion. As coordinator of student teachers in my school, I will be recommending that the teachers in training that I deal with should have a look at these videos.

DEB ('TAKE CONTROL OF THE NOISY CLASS' CUSTOMER)

"I found Rob Plevin's workshop just in time to save me from giving up. It should be compulsory – everybody in teaching should attend a Needs-Focused workshop and meet the man with such a big heart who will make you see the important part you can play in the lives of your most difficult students."

HEATHER BEAMES (WORKSHOP ATTENDEE)

"I have never enjoyed a course more, nor learnt as much as I did with Rob."

"What a wonderfully insightful, non-patronising, entertainingly informative day. I have never enjoyed a course more, nor learnt as much as I did with Rob. I was so impressed that I am recommending our school invite Rob along to present to all the staff so that we can all benefit from his knowledge, experience and humour."

RICHARD LAWSON-ELLIS (WORKSHOP ATTENDEE)

ABOUT THE AUTHOR

Hi, I'm Rob Plevin

I'm 51 years old. I live in the Eden Valley, Cumbria, with my wife, Sally.

We have three children between us, a dog called Bodhi and a pantomime horse called Ned.

I'm guessing that's not the kind of stuff you're looking for though; you probably want some credentials. Well, I'm an ex-special education teacher and even rose to the dizzying heights of 'Deputy Head' during the latter years of my career, although I much preferred being in the classroom with the kids. Since then, for the last 15 years, I've been running my own training company – training teachers, parents and carers in behaviour management and student motivation and, more recently, in mindfulness-based practices. I wrote this book because a lot of my work now involves working with parents and I believe activities like these are wonderful for cementing all-important parent-child relationships. You can contact me through my website at www.theliferaft.org.

Made in the USA
Middletown, DE
29 July 2021

45045811R00106